● Project UrbEx
● Ikumi Nakamura

● Project UrbEx
● Ikumi Nakamura

Adventures in ghost towns, wastelands
and other forgotten worlds

Foreword by Liam Wong

With over 400 illustrations

- Foreword by Liam Wong — p7
- The Road Less Travelled by Ikumi Nakamura — p8

● **North America**

01	Methodist Church	Pennsylvania, USA	p12
02	Sattler Theater	Buffalo, New York, USA	p16
03	Detroit	Michigan, USA	p22
04	The Island of the Dolls	Mexico City, Mexico	p34
05	Phoenix Trotting Park	Arizona, USA	p42
06	Planes in the Mojave Desert	California, USA	p46
07	Tonopah Hangars	Nevada, USA	p52
08	A Royal Blue Auditorium	New Jersey, USA	p56

● **Europe**

09	Powerplant IM	Charleroi, Belgium	p64
10	Oculus Tower	Ferrara, Italy	p70
11	Garment Factory	Central Italy	p78
12	Kupari Bay Hotels	Kupari, Croatia	p82
13	Petrova Gora Monument	Mali Petrovac, Croatia	p90
14	Manicomio di R	Piedmont, Italy	p94

● **Asia**

15	Village Clinics	Various rural areas, Japan	p104
16	Taman Festival Bali	Bali, Indonesia	p112
17	Imari Kawanami Shipyard	Kyushu, Japan	p118
18	N Amusement Park	Nara, Japan	p122
19	Wagakawa Plant	Iwate, Japan	p128
20	Garbage Disposal Plant	Japan	p132
21	Ikeshima Island	Nagasaki, Japan	p136

Project UrbEx

22	Niigata Russian Village	Niigata, Japan	p142
23	Bedugul Taman Hotel	Bali, Indonesia	p146
24	Houtouwan Fishing Village	Shengshan Island, China	p152
25	Gunkanjima	Nagasaki, Japan	p160
26	Hachijo Oriental Resort	Izu Islands, Japan	p172
27	Hokkaido Sex Museum	Jozankei Onsen, Japan	p176

● **Location Classified**

28	An Abandoned Villa	A quiet suburb, Europe	p182
29	Lumber Processing Plant	Deep in the jungle, Asia	p190
30	The Empty City	An industrial zone, Asia	p196
31	UFO Houses	A stormy beach, Asia	p202
32	Strange Cult's Bra Temple	In the mountains, Asia	p210
33	Soviet-era Flight School	A military base, Europe	p216

Foreword
Liam Wong

Many people will know Ikumi Nakamura the videogame developer, but her unseen talent as a photographer reveals another side that will both impress and disturb you in equal measure.

Ikumi remained anonymous for over a decade, hidden behind a gas mask. She was known as 'Tommy', an alter ego through which she could express herself in a way that she could not in her everyday life, as a photographer documenting her adventures on the website *Tomboy UrbEx*. As Tommy, Ikumi became a thrill-seeker in search of forgotten worlds, pushing her boundaries to feel alive while exploring abandoned, off-limits places as well as her own creativity.

Videogames have long been inspired by real-world locations. From the bustling streets of Tokyo's red-light district in *Yakuza*'s Kamurochō to Edinburgh's dark and atmospheric back alleys as seen in *Dishonored*'s Dunwall, game developers have found inspiration in all corners of the globe to create a sense of realism and immersion for players. The worlds we create have infinite possibilities, limited only by our imagination, and world-building is the key to creating a successful videogame – to making it both believable and enjoyable.

Ikumi's work is a testament to the power of photography to inspire new worlds that are visually stunning and unforgettable, transporting the player to places informed by reality. Her photographs capture the essence of the environments she has witnessed – spaces which are often forgotten, overlooked and unseen. These are more than just a record of neglected spaces, however; they are also a meditation on the nature of time and memory. She shows us the beauty that can be found in even the most desolate of places.

For many of us, videogames are a way to escape the real world. Through Ikumi's images we are reminded that reality exists beyond the controller, and it can be just as exciting and inspiring as the game worlds that we build. These photographs prompt us to be a little less afraid to explore the world around us, just as we do in videogames.

It's an honour to introduce to you *Project UrbEx* and the work of photographer Ikumi Nakamura, formerly known as 'Tommy'.

The Road Less Travelled
Ikumi Nakamura

Why do I travel the world to visit crumbling apartments, rusting factories and weed-covered theme parks? What's the appeal of crunching through broken glass and staring up at the sky through the shattered roofs of mouldy old buildings? Well, let me flip those questions around and throw them back at you. Why do you travel the world to stay in gorgeous, gleaming hotels with beautiful swimming pools, or to visit perfectly preserved historic monuments?

It's for the experience... right?

So I guess I love a different kind of experience. Why conform to the typical tourist itinerary when you can plot your own course through uncharted, abandoned territory? Embrace the road less travelled? Make lonely and forgotten places the main reason to depart your ordinary life?

Over the years, I've met locals and delved into the hearts of cultures that lie far off the beaten path. I feel that I've not just seen each country, I've truly lived in them. And that, my friends, is the essence of unique travel. That's 'UrbEx'.

I started my urban exploration adventures years ago, before the internet and smartphones gave everyone all the answers, all the time. I liked the challenge of finding places based on website rumours, or by guessing their location from the architecture or vegetation in photographs taken by an anonymous traveller. It felt to me like every trip was a modern-day treasure hunt.

Since I am Japanese and cannot speak English, I tended to stand out from other UrbEx participants. I discovered that the UrbEx community – and yes, one does exist, hidden away on the internet – is full of larger-than-life characters. A few are determined to protect their finds, while a miraculous number of open-minded explorers are keen to spread the word.

I tried to avoid that sort of noise, preferring to explore alone or with the few friends I feel comfortable with. But since people overseas kept paying too much attention to me, 'Tommy' was born. With her iconic gas mask, Tommy could appear in photographs without anyone ever knowing that the author of the *Tomboy UrbEx* blog site and the videogame developer Ikumi Nakamura were the same person.

With the release of this book, now everyone knows. Exploring abandoned places has given me the freedom to walk on the wild side, but it's also been the inspiration for my games. The stories of Tommy and Ikumi are interconnected because looking at pictures of abandoned places to inspire game development led me directly onto exploring real abandoned places. Two sides of the same coin.

I have become the rare game developer who has real-world experience of the chaotic, crumbling places that feature so heavily in open-world videogames. I know how to evade security patrols and find the spot on a perimeter fence where I can squeeze through, unseen. I appreciate what a powerful tool a drone is, not just because I've used one in a game level, but because I have sent one up to find the safest route across an actual cracked, sagging rooftop. I like to think that the UrbEx adventures of Tommy have made the environmental designs of Ikumi's games all the more immersive, exciting and believable.

I will never run out of places to see. I would love to stand in the ruins of a movie theatre deep in China's Taklamakan Desert or the remains of an old artillery battery in England.

00.01

00.02

8   Project UrbEx

00.01, 00.03 – 00.04
The Tommy persona has allowed me to record my adventures in anonymity, without affecting my personal and professional lives.

00.02
The tools of my trade, from travel essentials such as a passport to a camera, flashlight and, of course, the iconic gas mask.

I now have a young daughter who seems to have inherited the Tommy bloodline. When she is older, I hope to go exploring with her, although I am worried that my stamina will be no match for hers.

For now, I present this record of my journey so far. For readers of the *Tomboy UrbEx* blog, I give you new and expanded stories. For videogamers, I have tried to explain how my UrbEx experiences have shaped the online worlds I have helped to create. For those who would never dream of crawling into an old building through its sewer system, I have gone in for you and brought back the photographs for you to see.

But for those few of you thinking about starting your own UrbEx journey, I hope this book provides inspiration. The standard narrative is that mankind has done nothing but defile and destroy our world. I dispute that. I think the places that humans have built and then abandoned have their own unique beauty. The power stations, factories and apartment blocks we no longer use may not be palaces, but they are fascinating records of our time on the planet.

Come and experience them with me.

Ikumi 'Tommy' Nakamura

Introduction 9

Phoenix Trotting Park, p42

● North America
● 01-08

北米

解説

Methodist Church
Pennsylvania, USA

Safety in abandoned places isn't guaranteed, so urban explorers have to stay alert. Sometimes, the dangers are obvious – a terrifying drop, black pools of mystery liquid, rusted-out ladders. Other times, you have to trust all your senses.

In 2018, it was my sense of smell that I had to rely on. You can be alerted to many threats by sniffing the air, from toxic black mould on the walls to soft, rotten wooden floorboards waiting to trap you. But this was a powerful, foul smell that could mean only one thing – humans had been living here. For a long, long time.

I absolutely love abandoned churches. This one was built in the late 1860s as people moved to Pennsylvania to work as coal miners, then closed in 2004 after the people had drifted away again. From its beautiful brick exterior, I had expected a wonderful but faded Victorian-styled chapel, but everything inside was in a far worse condition than I had imagined. ▶01.04 And then that odour got stronger and stronger...

I slowly and carefully peeked inside the room and immediately saw a bed with a foot sticking out. Time to leave – only this entrance was blocked and I didn't see any other way out. Had someone got trapped? Was that a corpse?

I looked again and realized it was just a sock, not a foot. ▶01.08 Phew! Scared me for a second! But then I looked again and got the chills. A knife sticking out of a shelf. 'The Love Sex Bed' written on a wall. Heh... I'm really glad I didn't run into anyone here.

01.01

01.02

01.03

✕ Religious
※ Methodist Church
▣ Pennsylvania, USA
▓ 2018

01.01 – 01.02
The serene, saintly aspects of this church still existed in close-up. Some beautiful stained glass windows. A hymn book...

01.03 – 01.04
...but in the wide shot, time and weather had gone to work, blowing out sodden plaster and letting wood rot creep in.

12 Project UrbEx

North America

01.05

01.06

01.05 – 01.06
It was upstairs that things got interesting, as the religious imagery of the chapel gave way to more mundane living conditions.

01.07 – 01.08
Here, tucked away from view and bothering nobody, was the home of a formally homeless person. To look further felt like an intrusion.

14   Project UrbEx

01.07

01.08

North America

Sattler Theater
Buffalo, New York, USA

Commissioned by department store owner John G. Sattler, the Sattler Theater opened in 1914 yet was renamed the Broadway in 1920 in the first of a lifetime of transformations. By the 1960s, it was a mosque visited by Malcolm X, while from the 1970s onwards, it was used by various churches.

I found the Sattler standing alone on a city block that was mostly grassy weeds. ▶ The handsome brick buildings that would have formed the street it was built on have long gone, replaced by parking lots, storage units and gas stations, while the high-rise towers of modern downtown were visible a mile or so away. Times change but so, it seemed, do city centres.

The interior was rusted, crumbling and in a very poor condition. Metal stairs groaned when I stepped on them, while the flooded basement was a no-go area due to the unknown content of the still, probably toxic, water. ▶ (UrbEx note – powder falling like snow from the roof of an old building is never a good sign!)

Many historic buildings have a cultural and architectural significance to the identity of a community. The front of the Sattler had a banner promoting a heritage fund and, while I would love many of the places I have seen to be repurposed as community centres, art galleries or even residential and commercial spaces, I fear the challenges of cost and meeting modern safety standards would be an almost impossible barrier to ever restoring this lovely building.

▶02.01

▶02.02

02.01
Architect Henry Span designed over a dozen theatres in the early 20th century, all in Buffalo, New York and nearby Niagara Falls.

02.02
Oops! I didn't bring any rubber boots (or flippers) so the basement full of still and polluted water was off limits.

02.03
The wonderful circular skylight cast an impressive beam into the darkened auditorium, lighting the specks of dust that filled the air.

✕ Cultural/Entertainment
※ Sattler Theater
▣ Buffalo, New York, USA
▩ 2012

02.01

Project UrbEx

North America

North America 19

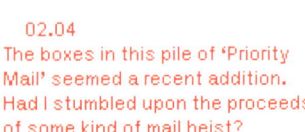

02.04

02.04
The boxes in this pile of 'Priority Mail' seemed a recent addition. Had I stumbled upon the proceeds of some kind of mail heist?

02.05
That skylight again. Without it, exploring this space would have relied on torches to reveal all the holes and jagged bits of metal.

02.06 – 02.08
Tommy risks sitting in a dusty, creaking chair to watch a performance of... nothing on an empty stage.

02.05

20   Project UrbEx

North America 21

解説

Detroit
Michigan, USA

I created the Tommy character so that I could visit empty buildings and Detroit really is ground zero for abandonment. It's one of the most beat-up, crumbling and yet beautiful cities I have ever seen, and one of the few places where almost an entire city packed up and moved elsewhere.

This birthplace of the motor industry lost over one million residents between the 1950s and the modern era as all the car factories shut down in rapid succession. The city doesn't just have single empty buildings, it has entire neighbourhoods that are abandoned or have burned down.

However, a lot of abandoned places in America are located in unsafe areas and Detroit has quite a reputation for being a dangerous place to get lost in. That's why, in 2012, I was super happy to be met in the city (after my fourteen-hour flight from Narita Airport) by a guide. Chris is a Canadian who explored Gunkanjima and Nara Dreamland with me in Japan and, without his support, this expedition would never have happened.

Straight away, it looked as if every building was a forgotten place and, while I think it might be rude to say, I quickly realized this was just America. Everywhere, I saw old cars driving on the roads and pedestrians with torn clothes walking down the streets. Even when we found a seedy, run-down motel on the outskirts to use as our exploration basecamp, it was surrounded by desolate streets of boarded-up buildings.
→p26

03.01

03.02

03.03

22   Project UrbEx

✕ Religious/Industrial/Domestic
※ Detroit
▣ Michigan, USA
▒ 2012

03.01 – 03.03
St Agnes' is a very grand church for its suburban location. It was used between 1924 and 1989 and has been badly vandalized.

03.04
The similarly large scale of the school next-door gives you some idea of how many people used to live round here.

03.05
The school's communal toilets stood dry and unused which, given the lack of plumbing, was something of a blessing.

North America 23

03.06
Community facilities were hard hit by the rapid depopulation of Detroit because when the people leave, these buildings no longer serve a purpose.

03.07
St Agnes Catholic School was established for the children of Ugandan immigrants by a parish congregation in 1917.

03.08 – 03.10
Closed after sixty years due to a lack of new students, the building has been stripped of plumbing, although books remain in piles.

Project UrbEx

North America 25

←p22
Many of the apparently derelict buildings were serving as makeshift shelters for the homeless, yet it was the few intact structures that caught our attention. In the shadows of towering factories left to decay, families with small children still lived in apartment buildings.

Over the next few days, I saw many of these. For just a mere $100, I could have bought a whole house – my very own piece of the city's rotting heart. Then there is the Brush Park Historic District – a twenty-four-block midtown neighbourhood designated by the city as a place of historic interest. Built in the French Renaissance Revival style, these Victorian-style homes would have once been exclusive dwellings for the rich. Yet these days, they are also on the verge of collapse.

But I went there to see Detroit's more famous empty buildings and one of my major missions was to sneak inside the Michigan Central Station. Built in 1912, it was well known as the tallest railway station of its time and, more recently, was a location for one of the *Transformers* movies.

Unfortunately, when we met another UrbEx adventurer, he said that increased security had made it extremely difficult, if not impossible, to sneak into the place. This was cruel news for me, and while I viewed it from behind a fence, it wasn't enough. Next time, for sure!
→p31

03.11
The Packard Automotive Plant built cars from 1903 to 1956, switching to aircraft engine production in the war years.

Project UrbEx

North America

03.12

03.13

28   Project UrbEx

03.14

03.15

03.12 – 03.13
The place was huge, employing 40,000 workers at one time. The scale of the place was mind-boggling.

03.14 – 03.15
The site was used for raves, as filming locations and even as offices until 2010, at which point it was finally abandoned.

03.16
Sadly, demolition of the site began in late 2022, so much of what you see here is already gone, with the rest to follow.

03.16

North America

03.17 – 03.19
I first visited these electric trams in 2015, then again in 2018, when I asked someone I was travelling with to get the drone shots.

Project UrbEx

03.03

03.11

03.20

03.17

←p26

We kept on moving and saw the sights, some big, some small. St Agnes Church, ▸ built in 1924, abandoned in 1989, with its own school next door. The vast Pontiac Silverdome, opened in 1975 with a giant fibreglass roof that was held up by pressurizing the air inside the stadium. And, even bigger than that, the 1907 Packard Automotive Plant, ▸ covering 325,000m² (3,500,000ft²), making it the largest abandoned place in the city.

We also saw the effect that the departure of so many Detroit residents had on surrounding areas. Outside of the city limits, the so-called 'Rust Belt' of post-industrial states stretches for hundreds of miles, leaving underpopulated towns, empty churches and even these unwanted railcars dotting the landscape ▸.

03.18

03.19

North America   31

03.20 – 03.21
I counted forty-five rusting streetcars, some still showing their route cards. Now they are lined up far out in the Pennsylvania woods.

32 Project UrbEx

03.22 – 03.23
In their time, they would have carried thousands – maybe millions – of workers heading to and from work in the city.

03.24
Think of the people hearing the hum of electric motors as this arrived every morning, then the click or hiss of the opening door.

North America 33

☼ Bizarre
※ The Island of the Dolls
▣ Mexico City, Mexico
▦ 2019

04.01
Despite the 'Welcome' sign, the warning that this isn't a typical tourist spot is tied to the fence.

04.02 – 04.04
Nailed onto fences and hanging from trees, thousands of dolls stare at you. It's very odd.

04.05
The island is one of Mexico City's many reclaimed swamp patches divided up by human-made canals.

34   Project UrbEx

解説 The Island of the Dolls
Mexico City, Mexico

▶04.05

▶04.11

Xochimilco is a borough of Mexico City that has 170km of canals linking little artificial islands called 'chinampas'. ▶ The story goes that this island's caretaker, Don Julián Santana Barrera, found a little drowned girl alongside her floating doll, which he recovered from the deep, clear waters and hung from a tree. But then, over the next fifty years, every time he returned to the island for a new work day, more dolls had appeared. ▶ The Island of the Dolls – *La Isla de las Muñecas* – had sprung into creepy life.

Is this the truth or the legend? And does it matter when the legend is such a great story? Don Julián Santana Barrera died in 2001 and the island has since become a popular tourist attraction, with a four-hour boat trip costing around 50 pesos.

Officially speaking, it is not an abandoned place at all and it's now so popular, there is also a fake Dolls Island on the way to the real one! Tourists sometimes get taken there by a 'bad' boat and charged an admission fee. Only the genuine Island of the Dolls has a caretaker and kitty cats acting as security guards.

→p40

North America

35

04.06

04.07

36   Project UrbEx

04.06 – 04.07
The canals are so central that they are a popular recreational spot for locals and tourists, supporting a fleet of boats.

04.08 – 04.10
Slowly swinging in the breeze, this many hanging dolls fill your mind with uncomfortable images of hanging corpses.

North America   37

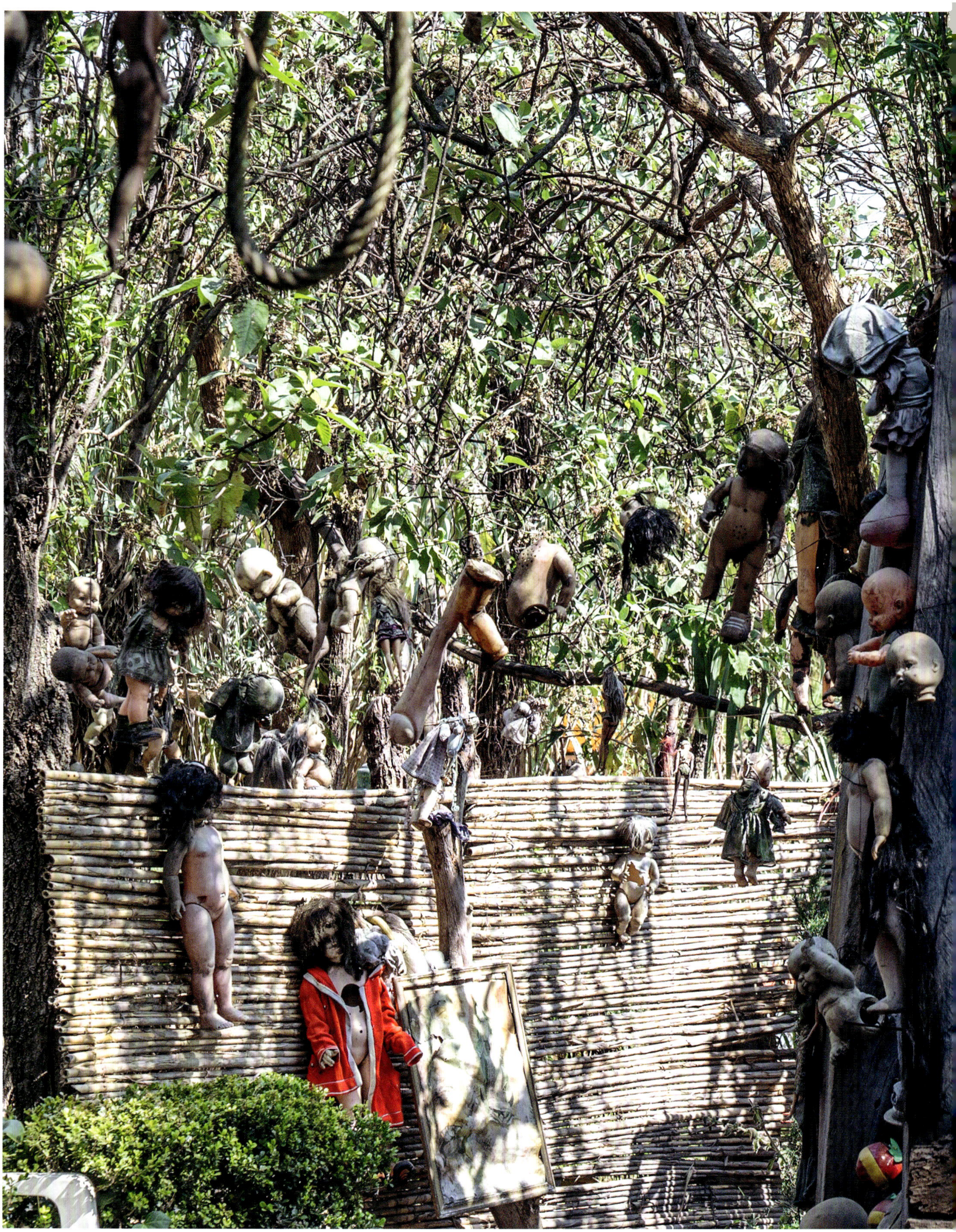

04.11
Dirt and moss complete the transformation from beloved toys to creepy nightmare fuel.

North America

←p35
I was impressed that my little boat was named after a woman, as they all were. Also, whenever we passed other boats, each one kindly offered tequila with fruit. I don't drink alcohol, but everyone else looked very relaxed and the Mexican cola I had was really tasty, since it's produced with local sugar cane.

I knew the history of this island before my visit, which made me feel a little sad, as if I was visiting a grave. The dolls all looked sad too, as if they wait forever for the return of the kind-hearted soul who created this island.

Yes, the staring, decaying dolls make the island reminiscent of a horror movie. But I found it far more horrific to go to the salaryman-style office building of a game company back when I had to commute to work every day. Haha!

40 Project UrbEx

04.12 – 04.13
In recent years, dolls have been at the centre of many popular horror movies and it's not hard to understand why.

04.14
This sign says, I think, something along the lines of 'Intruders will be hunted, gutted and torn apart.' It's a joke… I think…

04.15
…while this one translates (roughly) to 'Cursed content', as if the blue-eyed doll painted with blood splatter hadn't warned you.

North America 41

解説 Phoenix Trotting Park
Arizona, USA

I love movies, but the film industry once disrupted my UrbEx plans. On a trip to New Orleans, guards stopped me getting into an abandoned power plant because they were filming *Planet of the Apes*. Then, when I went to the nearby Six Flags amusement park, they were shooting a different film there. Oh, Hollywood!

But when I went to the Phoenix Trotting Park, I was fifteen years behind the film crew. This huge, futuristic horse racing track ▶ was opened in 1965 but immediately ran into problems and quickly closed. The Arizona desert was just too hot.

Years later, it was a location for the 1998 film, *No Code of Conduct*, starring Martin Sheen and his son Charlie. Search on YouTube and you can see the whole building swallowed up by such a fiery explosion that I could still see the scorch marks on the concrete years later.

Despite being remote, I encountered tighter security than most abandoned places. There was a high fence I couldn't climb over, although as I'm so petite, I could slip through the cracks.

The building had been vandalized but, walking around, it felt like being in a spaceship. The torn-apart central escalator was the best part. Beautiful. Take me to the Mother Ship.

It exists only in photographs now. The owners tried to sell it in 2015 for $16.5m but nobody wanted it and, sadly, it was torn down in 2017.

▶ 05.04

05.01

✵ Cultural/Entertainment
※ Phoenix Trotting Park
◉ Arizona, USA
✳ 2014

05.02

Project UrbEx

05.01
Even on my first visit, the remote setting hadn't protected this place from being mauled by vandals and scrap metal hunters.

05.02
But it got even worse. When a sale fell through, bulldozers moved in and, by October 2017, it was just rubble and memories.

05.03 – 05.04
Brand new and gleaming white in the desert sun, this would have been a stylish, yet ultimately impractical, sporting venue.

05.05 – 05.06
Every attempt was made to shield visitors from the heat, but it didn't work. The race track closed only a few years after it first opened.

North America 43

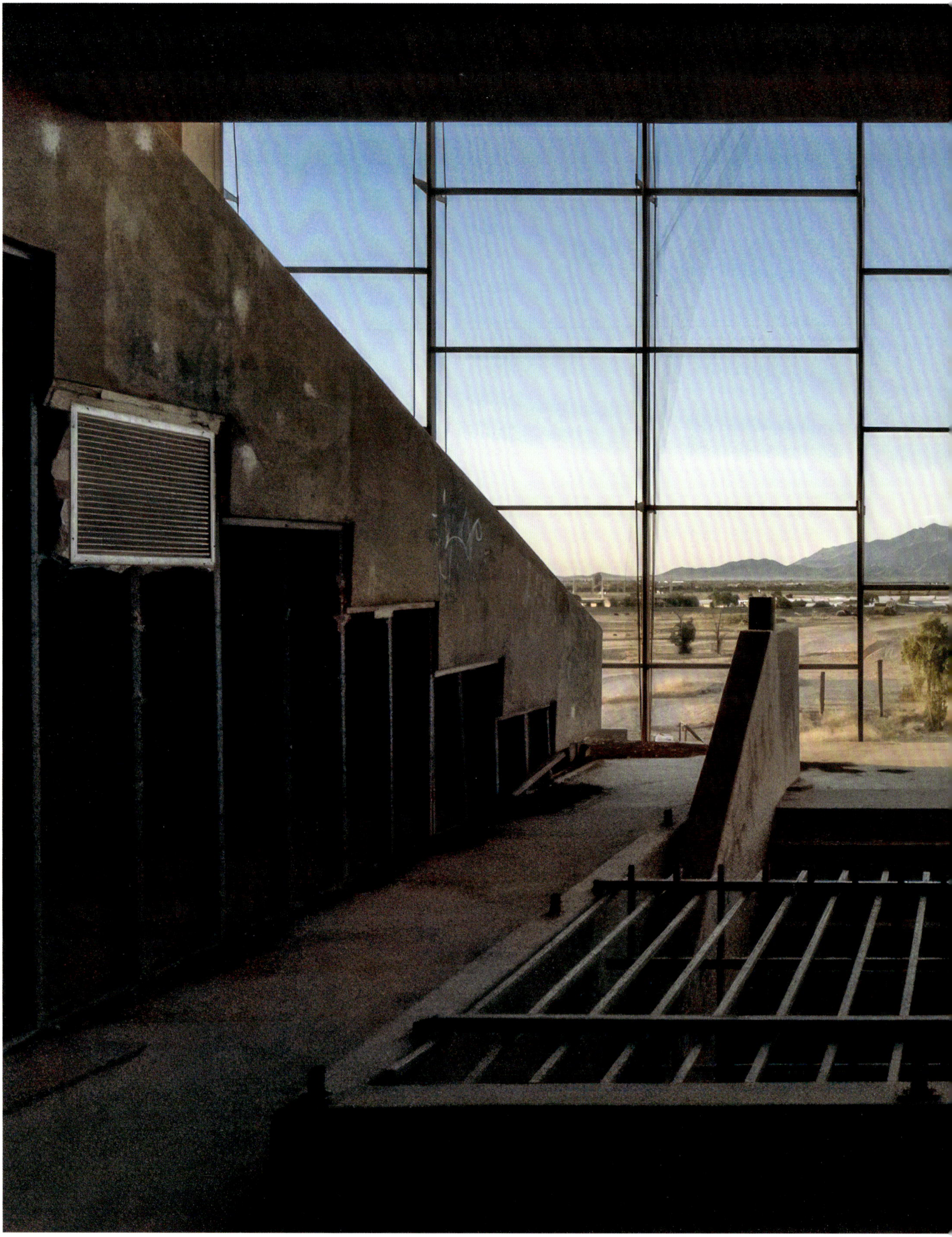

North America 45

解説 Planes in the Mojave Desert
California, USA

This is my favourite abandoned place and although I have visited three times, I am always thinking about making one more trip. The place has such a special atmosphere, with Edwards Air Force Base off across the desert, the silent, glowing engines of distant fighter jets taking off at night looking like UFOs.

Standing next to these wrecked planes has become a mystical experience for me, especially when the wind sighed through their thin metal skeletons. ▶ Arriving there at night and then seeing the sun rise over them was very moving. I wish I could have stayed there even longer.

▶06.04

Cars are not allowed out in the desert, so we hid ours in the grass and walked for about half an hour. I had heard stories about the Mojave Desert at night and was prepared for pitch black darkness and freezing winds, but on the night I went, I got the complete opposite. Not cold, no wind at all and the moon was shining brightly. ▶ A perfect night! It's so hard to put into words the quality of the sand lit bright by moonlight, although 'eerie beauty' comes pretty close.

▶06.09

I have loved fighter planes since I was a child, and when I saw *Top Gun* (the original) for the first time, I longed to be an air traffic controller so military planes would take off and land at my command. Imagine that kind of power!

46 Project UrbEx

✈ Military
※ Planes in the Mojave Desert
▣ California, USA
▩ 2017

06.01
In America, if it looks like a target, it becomes a target. Not many bull's-eyes though.

06.02 – 06.05
Despite its cute appearance, one of the many nicknames of the B-52 bomber is the 'death bird', making it a very attractive aircraft with contrasts. These were first built in the 1950s, but the US Air Force plans to use them into the 2040s and beyond – a full century of flight. I had missed the B-52 so much from my previous visit that when I spotted it, I yelled 'Ohisashiburi!' ('It's been so long!') and ran to it.

North America 47

06.06 – 06.07
From its exposed nose section to the gun turret in the tail, this B-52 looked incredible from every angle.

06.08 – 06.10
I will never get tired of that empty feeling you get out in the desert. Love emptiness. Yay emptiness. This place is so special to me that I will definitely return. I sat down on the plane and enjoyed this night from the top.

Project UrbEx

Random Observations on Global Urban Exploration #1

One day, I walked into a small church and interrupted a couple of homeless people making love there. They welcomed me in, but I was so embarrassed, I walked right out again. The church was filled with their possessions. It was their love nest.

Project UrbEx

'Abandoned buildings often aren't abandoned at all'

Detroit blurred the line for me between urban landscapes and abandoned places because so much of the city was both. My motel was on a street full of boarded-up buildings, but the longer I looked, the more I realized that many were still in use. In other parts of the city, low-income families lived quietly behind locked doors.

Random Observations

Xochimilco is so attractive that both residents of Mexico City and tourists flock there, supporting a local industry of colourful boats called '*trajineras*' that transport visitors around little islands called '*chinampas*'. So many beautiful Spanish words for a beautiful area!

Project UrbEx

'*Big city, small boats, drunken tourists*'

    Mexico City, a sprawling urban landscape, is broken up into sixteen boroughs known as '*demarcaciones territoriales*'. One such borough is Xochimilco, which has an identity very different from the rest of the city due to its network of canals and islands. The area was a lake that was drained over the centuries, and the waterways are now a World Heritage Site.

    My journey to the Island of the Dolls (see p34) was very festive, thanks to a lot of happy people drinking a lot of local alcohol. Not me though! Everyone waved and took photos of each other as our little '*trajineras*' passed by. Such a wonderful, sunny memory.

Random Observations

I'd been told that the site was patrolled by private security and that even a state trooper lived on the grounds. After I'd been inside, I saw the fresh tyre tracks of a patrol that had driven past me. It was pure luck I'd missed them! If my timing had been different, then what?

Project UrbEx

'So few visitors. So many guards!'
    The security surrounding the Phoenix Trotting Park in Arizona was both confusing and unnecessary. Built as a racing track in the 1960s, it had quickly shut down and endured years being vandalized. In the 1990s, an action movie filmed an explosive sequence there, but that was the only activity.
    Yet for some reason, this facility was locked down... tight! A double perimeter fence made me uneasy, because I had no idea how to get past it – although, as I'm so small, I just squeezed through a crack in the gate.

Random Observations

'I dream about fighter jets... now and forever'

If ever I travel to the United States, for work or for pleasure, I will do whatever it takes to see the planes in the Mojave Desert. It is my favourite abandoned place. I have been there three times already, and I am always considering a return trip.

I have loved fighter planes ever since I was a child, when I used to own plastic models of them. After I saw *Top Gun* for the first time, I realized I didn't want to fly like Tom Cruise, I wanted to be the marshal telling fighter jets to take off and land at my command. To be able to stand in the desert and actually touch such planes reignites that childhood dream.

Project UrbEx

North America 49

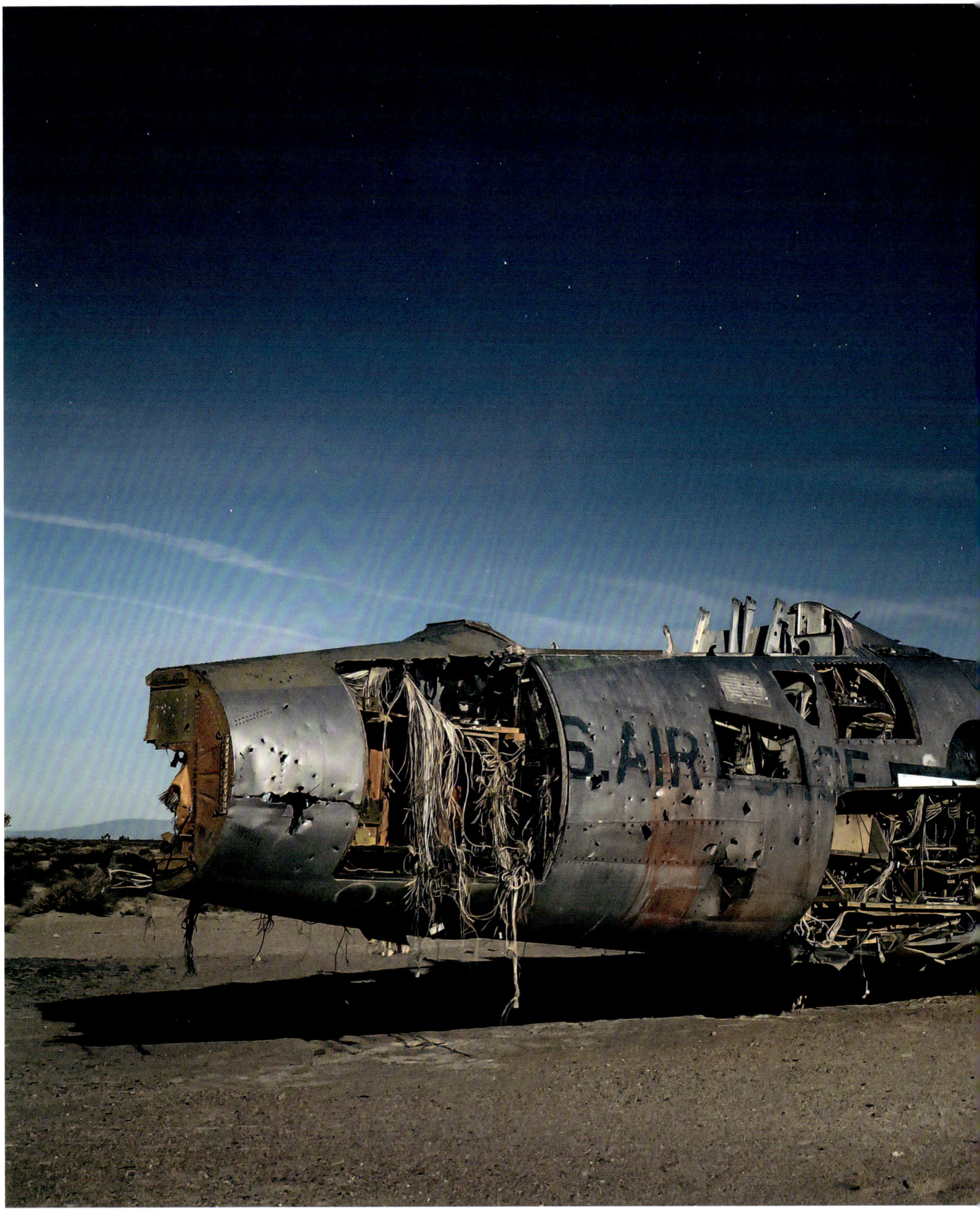
S.AIR

06.11
The F-101 Voodoo was a long-range fighter that entered service in 1959. This wreck looked less like a plane and more like a crash-landed spaceship.

North America 51

解説

Tonopah Hangars
Nevada, USA

The Second World War came suddenly to this corner of Tonopah, Nevada and departed just as quickly, leaving four giant wooden aircraft hangars to bake under the desert sun.

They were built as part of a training base for fighters, with US Air Force personnel arriving in July 1942. The base was then expanded a year later to house sixty-six bombers for crews to train on before they headed into combat over Europe and the Pacific. At its busiest, over 6,000 people lived on the base, while 134 pilots and crew died there in training accidents and crashes. But when the war ended in September 1945, it was abandoned almost overnight.

When I visited in 2017, three of the original hangars remained – the fourth having burned down some time earlier. It took five hours to drive to the site from Los Angeles. Not far by American standards but not close enough, either.

The runway is still in use as a civilian airport and of the three hangars, two were being used. Just one, to the south of the runway, was empty and accessible. ▶ Even though it was winter, the desert air was unbelievably dry. Exploration memo: always remember to pack a chapstick as a desert essential.

We stood in the absolute silence and gazed up at this incredible structure built over seventy years ago. It was designed only for wartime use, yet here it still was. Imagining all those beautiful planes going in and out of the building made me want to jump up and down in excitement, but that was before I spied a rusting classic car nearby. ▶

Eek!!! Wind-worn hangars, weathered vehicle and desert landscapes – what an awesome trio. Whoever you were, thank you for abandoning your car in such a great spot.

▶07.06

▶07.01

✕ Military
※ Tonopah Hangars
◉ Nevada, USA
※ 2017

07.01

52   Project UrbEx

07.01
Whoever left the truck here was just dumping trash, yet they inadvertently created some perfect Americana.

07.02
This was the only WW2 hangar that stood apart from the still-operating airfield, so it had been left to slowly fall apart.

07.03
Tonopah is incredibly hot. With only 12.5cm (5in) of rain annually, it must have been a dusty wartime posting for 6,000 personnel.

North America 53

07.04
The entire airbase, including barracks and runways, was built in 1940 at great speed for $3m, which sounds like a bargain.

07.05
One of the rules of the American West seems to be that every object left out in the desert MUST include bullet holes!

07.06 – 07.07
These hangars once roared to the sound of B-24 Liberators – a type of four-engined bomber that saw action over Europe and the Pacific.

54 Project UrbEx

North America

56   Project UrbEx

解説

A Royal Blue Auditorium
New Jersey, USA

Nothing felt safe about this old high school that I visited in 2018. Firstly, getting in was very easy... too easy. I remember being surprised that the doors were open and from that moment onwards, I was immediately on high alert. There is nothing more frightening than an abandoned place that's already open, since it increases the likelihood that someone else is already inside.

The neighbourhood around the school was very run down, which made me think that things must have been happier and more hopeful back when when they built the place. Think *Back to the Future*, only set in New Jersey.

All the classrooms had been built around the main auditorium ▶, so students must have been able to look out of their room and into this wide-open space.

Even in the decayed state that I found it in, I thought the auditorium was still absolutely gorgeous. Rays of light coming through a stained-glass ceiling made the royal blue seats glow. ▶ The star-spangled flag hanging in the auditorium screamed that this place was American. Faded, for sure. But patriotic to the very end.

▶08.07

▶08.01

08.01
Salute to the red, white and the very, very blue! While not everyone sees it, I find there's a certain beauty to the processes of decay in abandoned places.

08.02
That said, this auditorium would have looked magnificent at every point in its history, thanks to the vast space enclosed under its incredible stained glass ceiling.

✕ Cultural/Entertainment
※ A Royal Blue Auditorium
▣ New Jersey, USA
▦ 2018

08.02

North America

57

08.03

08.04

08.05

08.03 – 08.05
It still looked as though a deep clean could restore this space. A few more years of graffiti and decay would see it off, though.

08.06
Progress? The inspirational quote seemed slightly sarcastic now that it was on the peeling wall of an empty hallway.

08.07 – 08.08
What a spacious and airy school this would have once been, with windows opening onto the central auditorium from every side.

Project UrbEx

North America 59

Project UrbEx

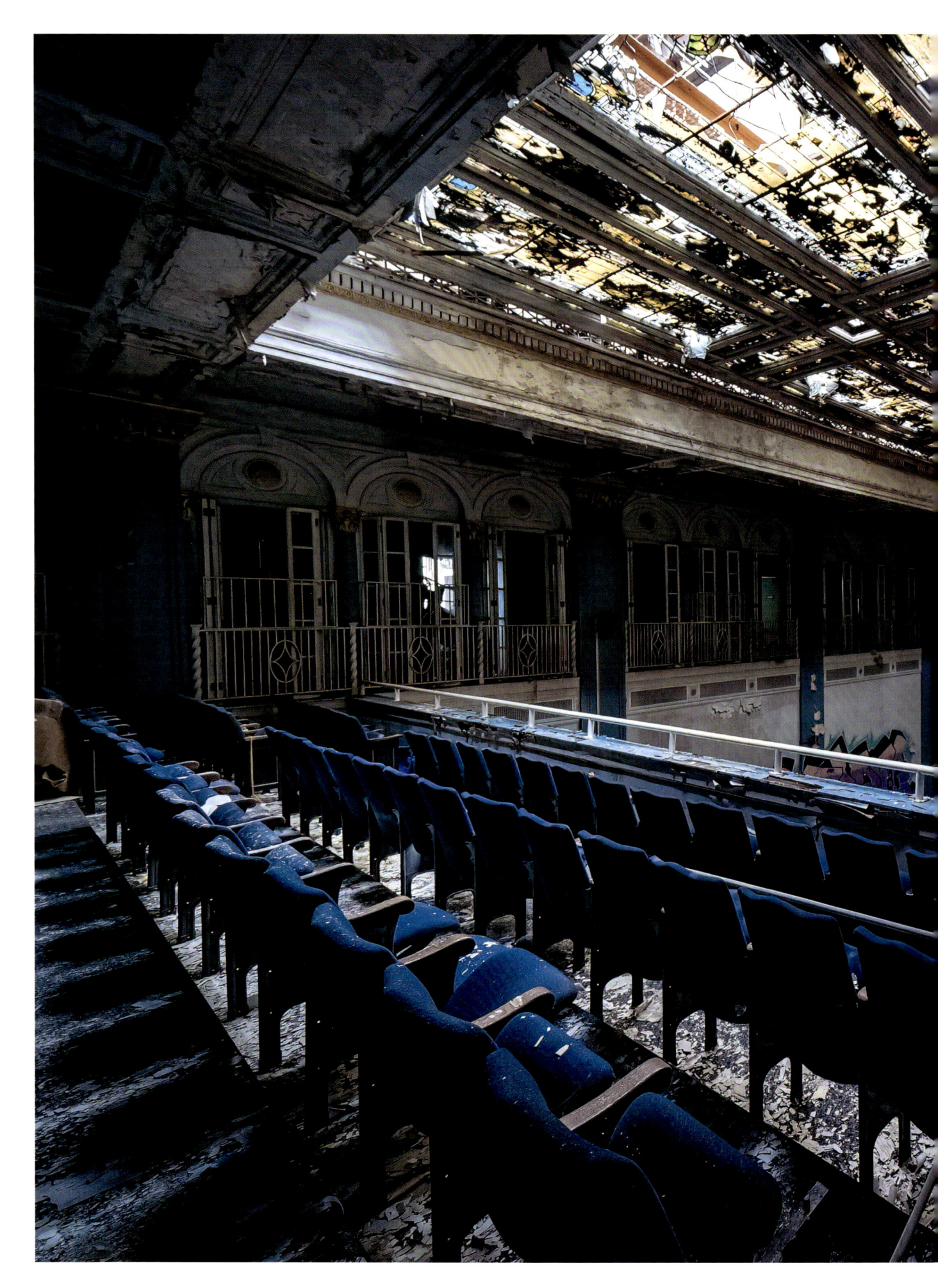

North America

Kupari Bay Hotels , p82

● Europe
● 09-14

ヨーロッパ

欧羅巴

解説 Powerplant IM
Charleroi, Belgium

Powerplant IM is, to my eyes, the coolest cooling tower in Europe. The Queen of Industrial Towers. I had been fascinated by pictures of it on the web for years, but it was only in 2014 that my wish to visit was realized. FINALLY!!!

Dominating a deserted factory district in Charleroi, the tower was part of a coal-fired power station built in the 1920s. It's so unusual that even today, people still travel from far and wide to come and look at its pioneering design. One hundred years ago, when it was first built, it must have looked very menacing and sci-fi as it cooled nearly half a million gallons of steaming water every minute, sucking in the cold surrounding air through the gaps around its base ▶ before endlessly blasting plumes of clouds high into the sky.

The Powerplant IM complex grew so big that by the start of the 2000s, it was responsible for 10% of Belgium's entire CO_2 emissions. All that heat and steam also encouraged dangerous pathogenic bacteria within the cooling tower's mossy, wet interior. ▶ To protect the health of the locals, the whole plant was shut down in 2007.
→p69

▶09.02

▶09.06

09.01

09.02

✕ Industrial
※ Powerplant IM
▣ Charleroi, Belgium
▩ 2014

09.03

64 Project UrbEx

09.01 – 09.02
The water-filled sub-level was hard to reach, but Tommy approves of the photo opportunity.

09.03
Did I say that this was big? I mean... really big? The visual impact is hard to overstate...

09.04
...and that's only from the outside. Once you stand at the bottom and look up? Mind blown.

09.04

Europe 65

66 Project UrbEx

09.05
While the powerplant was still operating, anyone standing here would have been steamed alive. Like a lobster.

09.06
Abandoned facilities that used to handle industrial volumes of water inevitably have terrifying concrete sluices and sinkholes.

09.07 – 09.10
The channels spread the boiling water across the base of the cooling tower, creating the billowing clouds above it.

Europe 67

68　　　　　　　　　　Project UrbEx

←p64
The moss was still there when I went in through a useless broken gate and up some old stairs. Inside, a deep, deep hole, covered by green and plunging down. The curved concrete sides of the tower going up and up and up. A beautiful and mysterious atmosphere.

And under the tower, a hidden level like a Final Boss stage. It was a bit hard to access because the route was flooded. But the view once you got underground? Priceless.

Europe

解説 Oculus Tower
Ferrara, Italy

In 2015, we implemented the 'Italian Invasion Plan'. This was a drive from northern to central Italy as part of an UrbEx trip that took in every abandoned place we knew about. As a side mission, we also rediscovered the charm of Italy by seeing the towns and mountain passes that regular tourists miss entirely. *Italia, veloce, veloce!*

Several years before, I had seen photographs of the Oculus Tower but never worked out where it was. Many explorers since have described it like this – 'Fantastic building!!' and 'One of the best places ever!!!'. With that many exclamation points in the reviews, I knew that OKAY!! Here we go!!!

This factory had been used for processing sugar beets into sugars for alcoholic drinks such as Martini, but with the urban population around the factory increasing over time, the government shut it down in 2003 due to environmental and air quality concerns.

One of the highest and most remarkable buildings is the Oculus Tower, which encloses a huge, airy space thanks to stairs curving around its perimeter and some amazing, tall windows. ▶ From these, I could look out over the rest of the factory. But just as I was planning to explore further...
→p76

▶10.08

10.01

10.02

10.01 – 10.02
It's just a concrete industrial plant, yet somehow, Italian architects had built in some incredible design elements that made it so cool.

10.03 – 10.04
The tower stood out both for its height and its incredible form. It drew me in from a distance and I knew I had to see inside.

10.05
With its production plant and storage vats, the factory looked like a great place to explore, but I only got to enter the main tower.

Project UrbEx

✄ Industrial
※ Oculus Tower
▣ Ferrara, Italy
▓ 2015

10.03

10.04

Europe   71

Project UrbEx

Europe 73

10.06
As is often the case in huge factories, the human-sized door looked tiny and out of scale...

10.07
...especially compared to the almost cathedral-like vastness of the tower's interior.

10.08 – 10.09
With exterior walls made almost entirely from windows, Oculus Tower resembled a concert venue.

Project UrbEx

Europe 75

←p70
...we saw five very suspicious guys. Carrying chainsaws. So what's the plan for two small UrbExers to deal with five giant *Gears of War* characters stealing metal from a factory? Specifically, five characters with chainsaws.

Did we run away? Yes we did.

So on that occasion, we only saw the tower and skipped the tour of the rest of the factory. But even from this shortened trip, it was clear that the Italian inclination towards aesthetic splendour is truly remarkable.

The incorporation of stunning design into even their industrial structures highlights the country's commitment to creating visually striking environments. The tower's unique 360-degree light penetration produces an ethereal ambiance that distinguishes it from pretty much every other functioning factory unit in the world.

We might have only seen the Oculus Tower this time. But it was definitely worth it.

10.10
Look out! Holes in the floors, missing safety rails and long drops all kept this UrbExer keenly aware of her own mortality.

Project UrbEx

Europe

解説 Garment Factory
Central Italy

This small-town garment factory had been closed for perhaps thirty years before I found it – since the middle of the 1980s, I think – so the many clothing items still there looked outdated to me. They must have been very fashionable in their time, though.

I think it takes about five years for an abandoned place to look like a museum or a ruin. If the rain gets in, some places evolve as vegetation encroaches, bad kids wreck it, and graceful decay takes place.

Other places, like this factory, remain protected from the elements so that, over the years, different factors slowly and silently go to work. Here, I found dust layered on top of threads and spider webs that were very fragile and beautiful. The machine underneath it all looked like the halo of Mary. ▶11.06

There were so many objects that told a history about this place and the lives of its employees. Not just sewing machines but the tools that repaired them and the clothing that was manufactured on them. ▶11.10 And in the office, old furniture, a dressing table and even bottles of liquor.

I had started my UrbEx blog before *The Last of Us* came out on PlayStation 3, so when I first played it, I felt that it showed slices of a world I was already familiar with. A world where, like in this factory, time had suddenly stood still. Maybe I'm being self-conscious, but I even wondered whether perhaps *The Last of Us* dev team had referred to my photos for some of their locations.

I've never encountered zombies or clickers, of course. But you can experience a similar situation by bumping into a human guard. It's still scary.

Project UrbEx

⋈ Industrial
※ Garment Factory
▣ Central Italy
▦ 2015

11.01 – 11.02
Like a museum to the industry of the 1980s, only dust, spiders and myself seem to have gotten in here.

11.03 – 11.05
So why could I still hear sewing machines? My brain filled in the sounds it wanted to hear.

Europe

11.06 – 11.08
Dust and cobwebs had caught on the threads still wound into some machines, adding cloud-like auras.

11.09 – 11.10
Clothes from the era that were never worn, alongside machines that will never be used again.

11.06

11.07

11.08

80　　　　　　　　　　Project UrbEx

11.09

11.10

Europe

✕ Tourism
※ Kupari Bay Hotels
◉ Kupari, Croatia
▦ 2016

12.01 – 12.02
Hotel Goricina sits within the vast Kupari Bay complex, once a world-class resort boasting beautiful beaches and clear waters.

12.03
Inside the Grand Hotel, it's easy to see why this place attracted tourists from all over the world, with its views across the bay.

82　　　　　Project UrbEx

解説 Kupari Bay Hotels
Kupari, Croatia

As I watched the old man walk down to the sea, I thought to myself, 'I should have stayed here, not in Dubrovnik.' Beautiful sky, clear blue ocean and huge hotels around the bay – what an amazing place for a holiday resort. But the hotel lobbies were silent apart from when debris toppled from broken roofs. And the grandfather in swimming trunks was carefully stepping down a slope because the shattered steps had been washed away by years of high tides.

Many explorers who face these crumbling hotels must shout, 'Too big! Too vast! Where do I go from here?' It's hard to know because this used to be a huge, high-class resort. But when civil war tore Yugoslavia apart in 1991, Croatian police took over this area, warships besieged the bay, and this beautiful resort became rubble in the twinkling of an eye.

Hotel Pelegrin ▸12.13 was built in the 1960s with over four hundred beds. When war came, it was attacked with missiles and guns. The holes in its walls told me how furious the battle had been. Behind it, the Kupari. ▸12.12 One of the resort's largest buildings was now more jungle than hotel. It must have burned fiercely many years ago, I thought, since I could still see blackened walls in many places.

Then there's the Grand Hotel, ▸12.04 built in 1919 with an uninterrupted view over the entire bay. It used to be the resort's most luxurious hotel, but when the shelling started in October 1991, its panoramic view made it an easy target.

We heard that a Turkish investor was making plans to rebuild this resort, but where would they even start the clean-up operation? Too big! Too vast! Where do they go from here?

12.01

12.03

Europe

12.04
Up close, though, most of the buildings bear the marks of those terrifying, violent moments in the 1990s that blew this place apart.

12.05
The bay must have been an incredible sight at the height of its popularity, with motion, music and laughter everywhere.

12.06 – 12.07
The fact that it was built for thousands of tourists made the isolation even stranger – I saw just a few people all day.

Project UrbEx

12.06

12.07

Europe

12.08

12.09

12.10

12.08 – 12.09
Knowing what happened here, these concrete structures often felt like bunkers rather than holiday facilities.

12.10 – 12.12
The Kupari Hotel seemed to be the biggest building – an almost endless poured-concrete maze where even the pool had a view.

86   Project UrbEx

Europe

12.13

12.14

88　　　　　　　　　　　　Project UrbEx

12.13
Hotel Pelegrin was designed in 1963 to be a giant, sealed glass-and-concrete building facing the full force of the ocean.

12.14 – 12.17
Every window is broken now, of course, the bullet holes and burns in the walls a record of the violent struggles that raged around it.

Europe

✕ Cultural
※ Petrova Gora Monument
◉ Mali Petrovac, Croatia
▓ 2016

Project UrbEx

解説 Petrova Gora Monument
Mali Petrovac, Croatia

I visited Croatia in 2016 to explore this monument as well as the hotels of Kupari Bay, which feature in the previous section. As with many parts of the former Soviet Union, Croatia has some big, bold war monuments that you wouldn't find anywhere else. The full name for this one is '*Spomenik ustanku naroda Banije i Korduna*', which translates as 'Monument to the uprising of the people of Kordun and Banija'.

It honours the local peasants who, in 1942, attacked armed militia fighters using only farm implements. Since this name is too long in any language, most now call it the 'Petrova Gora monument' after its site on Peter's Mountain.

▶13.01 Completed in 1981, the monument is made of concrete with stainless steel walls. ▶ This, I think, makes it a building rather than a statue. It looks like a space station from any angle, with wind gusting across the mountaintop making the sheet metal vibrate with strange, otherwordly shrieks.

The troubled 1990s saw civil war, death and widespread devastation across the entire region. Monuments were neglected as the country concentrated on rebuilding its infrastructure and, even now, the site continues to be damaged, with its valuable stainless steel ripped off to be sold ▶13.07 by the locals as scrap metal. ▶

Along with its unique design, I found this nihilistic building to be overwhelming. Despite the clear sky, it was so very eerie and mysterious.

13.01
Is it a spaceship, a statue, a building or the base of an evil genius? From every angle, it could be all of the above.

13.02
I could only imagine how dazzling this approach would have been when all the stainless steel panels were in place.

13.02

Europe 91

92　　　　　　　　　　Project UrbEx

13.03
The path leading to the monument on the hilltop is designed so that your attention is focused on it.

13.04
The People's Collective of Tommy meets the former Union of Soviet Socialist Republics.

13.05 – 13.07
Anything not bolted to a wall had been stolen, along with the steel sheeting which HAD been bolted!

Europe

解説 Manicomio di R
Piedmont, Italy

How many architecturally important old asylums are there in Italy? During my trip across the country in 2015, I visited two, both amazing me with their beautiful appearances. One had been part of an old ducal palace, no less, along with other parts of a neighbouring Dominican convent. This one – Manicomio di R – had been built around an old military college in the 1870s to house nearly four hundred patients.

These days, '*manicomio*' is taken to mean 'mental institute'; in older, crueller times, the more accurate translation would have been 'mad house'. This held dangerously violent patients alongside frail people with dementia until more modern, caring regimes created separate spaces for people with such different conditions.

This segregation created an enlarged asylum with nine hundred patients that was so huge, I spent five hours inside and still didn't manage to see everywhere. ▶ Being located downtown, it was difficult to get inside without being seen, but because I'm great at *Call of Duty*, I did plenty of sneaking and crawling through some dark and narrow holes.

→p101

▶14.09

14.01

14.02

94 Project UrbEx

⚕ Hospitals/Facilities
※ Manicomio di R
◉ Piedmont, Italy
▓ 2015

14.01 – 14.03
This abandoned psychiatric hospital was built around an old military college. How could one place have so much history!?

14.04
Or so many goats!? The story of my encounter with these animals is told in Random Observations #2.

14.05
Patients were both detained and treated here for nearly a century. If walls could absorb feelings, these would be crying.

Europe

14.06

14.07

96 Project UrbEx

14.06
This empty space still retained a sense of its former grandeur as I looked down from a high balcony.

14.07
I couldn't get to every part of the building, but the goats didn't seem to have a problem.

14.08 – 14.10
Serene and comforting or lonely and oppressive? These spaces were both at the same time.

14.11
A place for everything. This huge filing cabinet had been emptied of a hundred years of secrets.

Europe

Project UrbEx

Europe

14.12 – 14.13
Knowing the purpose of this place, it's impossible not to wonder about the people who spent so many years here.

14.14 – 14.15
Working within the videogame industry, it's also impossible not to think of all the levels that have used similar settings...

14.16
...and wonder whether a half-complete human skeleton had been left here simply to scare off timid explorers!

100 Project UrbEx

14.15

←p94
Some rooms were covered with white tiles and still housed pieces of medical equipment and incredible machinery, so it was impossible not to think about the procedures that patients would have endured. Yet the hallways had beautiful, high ceilings with graceful arches, and when the sunlight and vegetation were pouring in through broken windows, it was easy for me to forget the original purpose of this place.

A real surprise was how many goats there were. Yes... goats. Their life was full of freedom, wandering around the asylum, chewing grass and staring silently at the occasional UrbEx visitor. Someone told me that Italians often use goats for site security... do you know if that's true? I left them alone and they left me alone, too.

After over a century of use, Italy decided that large 'mad houses' like this one were no way to treat vulnerable people, especially since electroshock therapy and even operations on the nervous system were still being used. Italy's asylums were shut down in the 1980s, leaving behind many beautiful buildings with strange, sad pasts.

14.16

Houtouwan Fishing Village, p152

● Asia
● 15–27

亞細亞

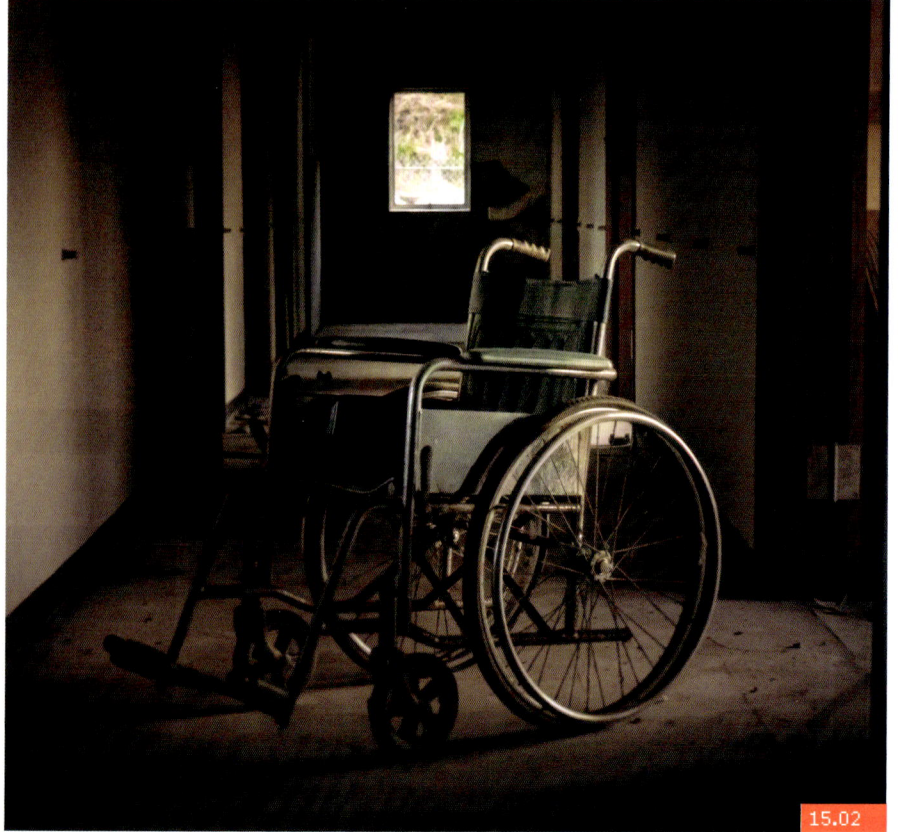

⚕ Hospitals/Facilities
※ Village Clinics
▣ Various rural areas, Japan
▦ 2014

15.01
It's hard not to think of all the life-changing moments that happened inside here.

15.02
For instance, at some point, the very last patient ever to use this was wheeled to the front door.

15.03 – 15.04
Likewise, this equipment was prepared for a procedure or operation that never happened.

104   Project UrbEx

解説 **Village Clinics**
Various rural areas, Japan

Without information on each site, it is difficult to say why these clinics in the Japanese countryside shut down. They all date to the Taisho era – a period between 1912 and 1926 during which Japan underwent significant political and social change, including the rise of democracy. Back then, such small health clinics would have been an important part of rural communities. Perhaps too many villagers moving to the cities caused their closures. Maybe the doctors simply retired or passed away.

There were many valuable items left in all of the health clinics that I visited, not just decades-old medical equipment ▶ but also medicines and even an ancient television. Why had one doctor left without framed portraits of their family? It was as if the owners had only just stepped outside for a minute.

→p106

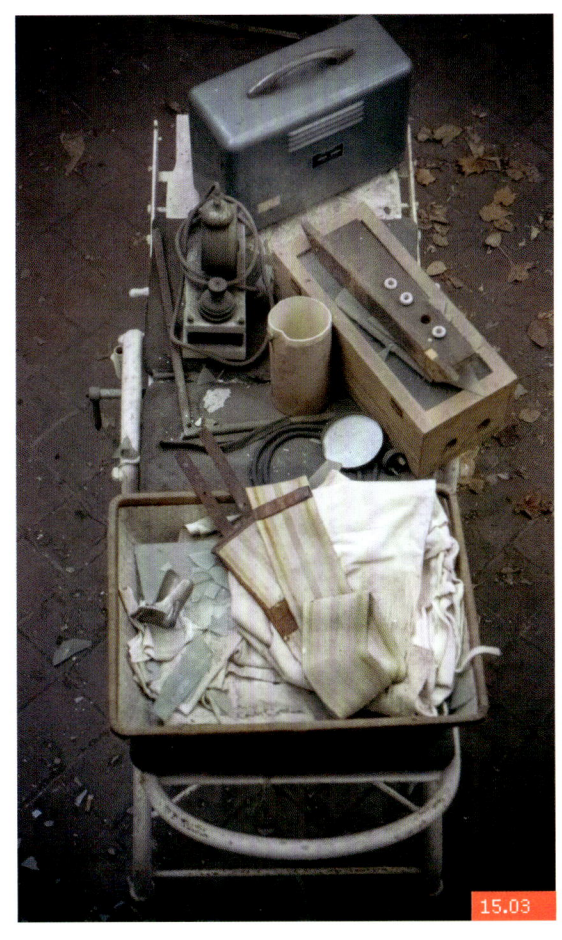

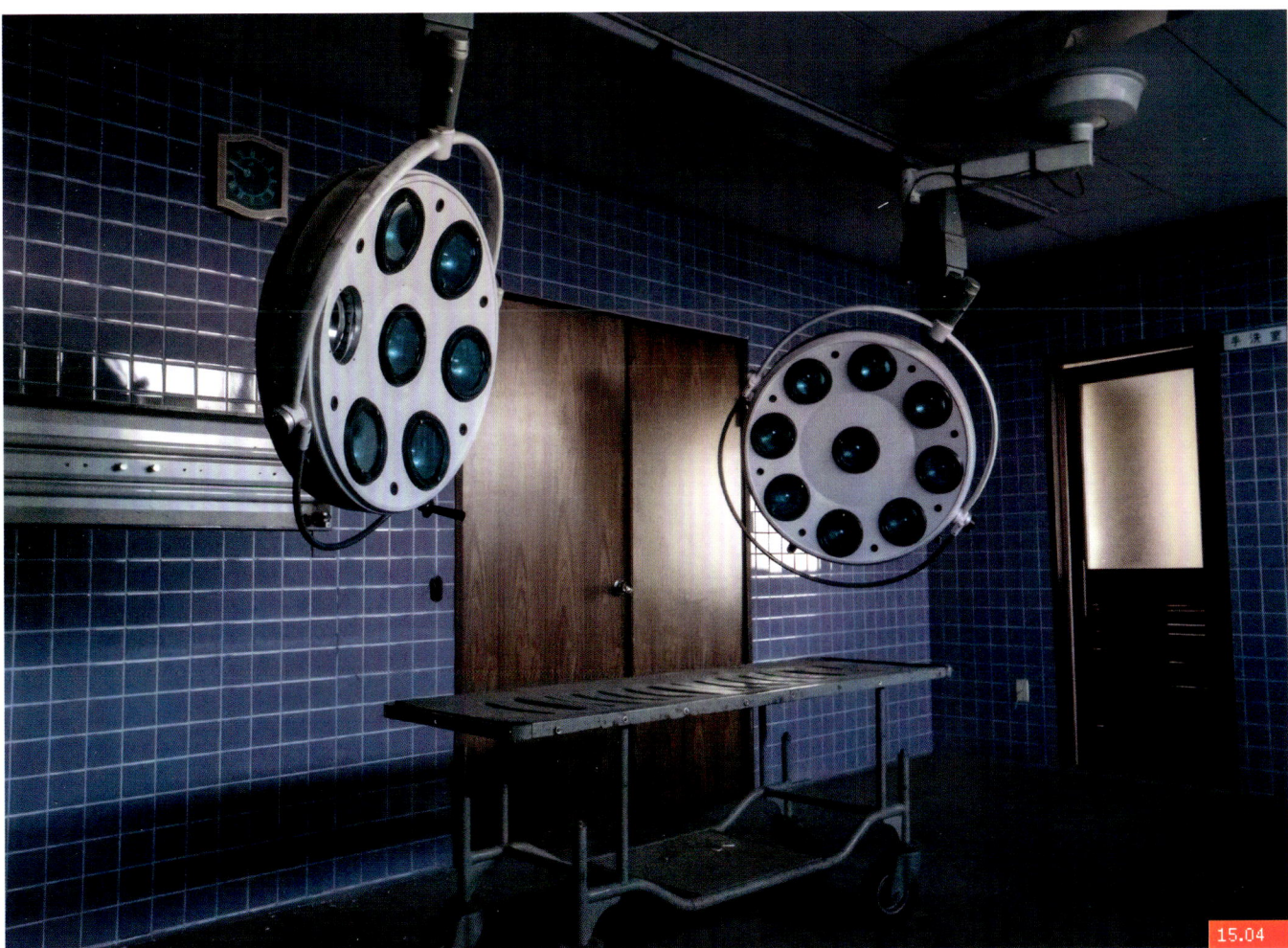

▶15.13

Asia

105

15.05 – 15.06
In their time, local clinics such as this one would have been an important asset for villages.

15.07
Now they are the domain of Tommy and other UrbExers, each one careful to disturb nothing.

15.08 – 15.09
The preservation within these abandoned clinics was amazing, with objects left everywhere.

106   Project UrbEx

←p105

The notion that beauty lies beneath the surface and slowly reveals itself is a prevalent concept in architecture and design. As they weather over time, structures can transform, affecting both their external and internal appearance. The rich, oxidized patina that adorns metal surfaces or the distinct polishing or wear that arises from daily use could be seen by some as rust or erosion. But to others, it can be quite beautiful.

With their ragged, 'Old Japan' architecture, overgrown gardens and faded patient charts, these clinics instantly evoked my childlike spirit of discovery. One of the attractions of abandoned hospital buildings is the smell. I explored these eagerly, intoxicated by the smells of disinfectants and chemicals. The region's high humidity had also rotted all the floors, making each step a dangerous but exciting game.

I often think many UrbExers feel like they are the protagonist in a horror game like *Silent Hill* or *Resident Evil* each and every time they explore an abandoned hospital! Such empty places, where life and death intersect, are certainly a rich source of inspiration for my game creation.

15.07

15.08

15.09

Asia

107

15.10
Alumigel for gastrointestinal ulcers? With a 'best before' date likely before I was born, I'll pass.

15.11
Are those the same spectacles from the ID photo? If so, what an amazing link to the past.

15.12
Are these the doctors from the surgery, their mentors or their relatives? We'll never know.

108 Project UrbEx

15.13
Visiting these clinics was as close to time travel as I'll ever get – glimpses into a world gone by.

15.14
How else can you describe standing in a room like this that's exactly as it was decades ago?

15.15
Or looking at pills, potions and powders that were made in long-closed clinical laboratories?

Asia

15.16
The region's humidity had taken a terrible toll on the wooden floors. Many boards looked fine but were dangerously rotten.

15.17
The reproduction Venus de Milo was an unexpected addition to an otherwise ordinary living room. At least I think it was a reproduction!

15.18 – 15.20
From cracks in the paint to mould in the wood and rust on the medical equipment, these clinics were all slowly decaying.

15.16

15.17

110   Project UrbEx

15.18

15.19

15.20

Asia

解説

Taman Festival Bali
Bali, Indonesia

Taman Festival Bali in Padang Galak cost $100m to build in 1998 and featured a roller coaster, a 3D movie theatre and Bali's largest swimming pool. But it's incorrect to call it an 'abandoned' theme park, since it never actually opened to the public. No one knows why.

Its decaying buildings and statues have since been swallowed up by nature, with the park's original topography seemingly designed to encourage explorers like me. The level design was so immersive, it turned me into a real-life Nathan Drake, embarking on an adventure through the captivating world of *Uncharted*. Playing that game made me feel I was in an imagined place I could never visit. Taman Festival Bali made me feel I was visiting a place that should have been in a game.

As an environmental artist, I visited some abandoned places so that the experience could help me create the visuals, textures and settings of *The Evil Within*. But what I've since found most helpful for game development is the actual experience of exploration. Being there allows you to feel like a game player in the real world. You can invade abandoned places while activating 'stealth mode'. I even use a drone to get a view of some sites from above so that I can safely infiltrate them, which feels a lot like another common game mode. I think I am a rare game developer who has experienced all this for real.

There are so many things I have learned from exploring abandoned places. It has kept the flame of my curiosity burning. It also requires me to communicate with a community of trusted explorers, since they often have the information or support that I need to tap into. This spirit of open-mindedness is what I value most because that, too, is a valuable skill in game development.

▶16.08

✕ Cultural/Entertainment
※ Taman Festival Bali
▣ Bali, Indonesia
▨ 2020

16.01–16.04
This site has been rediscovered by local people as a blank canvas for street art, with magnificent examples of all styles of graffiti on almost every surface.

16.05
Not so much abandoned as never occupied in the first place, this theme park was built at great expense but never even opened to the public.

16.06–16.10
The videogame vibe was strong in this place, with the slightly artificial theme park settings blending with the lush plant life to create perfect game zones.

112   Project UrbEx

Random Observations on Global Urban Exploration #2

Even if the goats had started out as farm animals, they had at some point been left to fend for themselves and had quickly become wild, with their offspring born feral.

Project UrbEx

'Abandoned places: where shoes go to die'

    I wasn't expecting the Manicomio di R asylum in Italy to be home to so many animals, let alone an entire flock of curious goats. The asylum, founded in the 1870s to house nearly four hundred patients, was quite beautiful inside. It struck me how easy it was to forget the original purpose of such a place.

    At some point in the past, the goats seem to have been released into the asylum's grounds – there was plenty of grass for them – so that the ruins would not be swallowed up by weeds. So we could thank all of these goats for constantly munching on the green stuff, and preventing this beautiful building from being covered by plants.

    However, the thick, deep carpet of goat droppings produced over the years created fresh problems for explorers. My shoes were never quite the same again.

Random Observations

While I was walking through Hotel Goricina, I came across two bulky guys taking the building apart for scrap metal. 'We're treasure hunting! Wanna join us?' they asked me. Since I only ever take photographs, I shook my head and left them to it.

Project UrbEx

'Abandoned places have an irresistible appeal to all kinds of people'

In the 1990s, the massive Kupari luxury resort in Croatia was briefly the scene of several intense battles during Yugoslavia's civil war, which left the whole area scarred, battered and abandoned.

A few years after I explored it, the area was also used as a location for the music video of a track called *Darkside* by a famous DJ named Alan Walker. I can never know whether he'd looked at my blog site or not, but the illustration below expresses my self-consciousness that I may have inspired him.

Perhaps, like many filmmakers, they were drawn to the unique nature of a place that was so suddenly abandoned. It had been used right up until the moment that calamity arrived, like a localized apocalypse.

ALAN WALKER BETTER BE CHECKIN' OUT MY PICS AND PICKIN' A SPOT.

OVERLY SELF-AWARE

Random Observations

Being lost in an abandoned place, like a mouse trapped in a maze, can be a little bit frustrating. But a drone can look down and create a real-time map, with me in the middle looking up at it.

Project UrbEx

'A bird's-eye view is a wonderful thing. Magical, even'

Hobby drones have only been around for a few years, but already it's hard to imagine ever being without them. Before drones, aerial shots for film or TV productions were rare because each one would have required a fully fuelled helicopter, two pilots and a cameraperson. Yet these days, even the presenters of a local news report can throw a drone up into the air!

I have found many uses for drones in my UrbEx adventures. Obviously, I can take photographs of sites from high above or even looking at them from across stretches of open water, which would be impossible for me to access. But I can also gain information about abandoned places from the air so that, even before I start to explore for the first time, I have already planned a safe infiltration route.

And in what feels very much like a videogame mode, I have even used a drone to get out again!

Random Observations

IT'S LIKE 'THE LAST OF US'!!!

Words often uttered by ruin explorers who like to play videogames.

Project UrbEx

Asia

16.06

16.07

Project UrbEx

16.08

16.09

Asia

Project UrbEx

Asia

解説 Imari Kawanami Shipyard
Kyushu, Japan

Kawanami Shipyard was on the outskirts of Imari at the southern end of Japan. I visited in 2007, then again in 2010, shortly before the site was demolished. This was at the start of my UrbEx adventures, when I was a rookie explorer in an all-girl expedition. We were new to everything. Built in 1851 as a glass factory, this site became a busy shipyard and munitions factory during the Second World War, before closing around 1950.

We visited the night before to calculate the best time and route to infiltrate. Sounds like a game, right? We quickly realized that since it was an accessible location, many people had visited, even the bad kids from the neighbourhood. I was most surprised to find some pink panties ▶ left on the second floor... What!? They looked glorious.

You might think that abandoned places feel gloomy, but I remember this being the ultimate in decadent beauty. Full of light, trees, the smell of fresh air. All human-made objects return to nature. When we die, we too become dust and soil.

As proof of this, two weeks after my second visit, a body was found here. It was a suicide by hanging and they had been there for a month, so apparently I had walked right under the body. I felt sorry that I didn't notice.

The shipyard has gone now. I remember seeing rules painted on a wall ▶ and could sense the men and women who built ships in wartime. This was a valuable page from history that should have been preserved.

▶ 17.08

▶ 17.01

✕ Industrial
※ Imari Kawanami Shipyard
▣ Kyushu, Japan
▩ 2007, 2010

Project UrbEx

17.01
'Attention Workers!' This hand-painted sign from the Second World War was still clearly legible.

17.02
Despite looking remote, the city and road were both nearby, their familiar sounds in the background.

17.03 – 17.07
As with most of the semi-tropical places I have visited, vegetation was growing vigorously.

17.03

17.04

Asia 119

17.05

17.06

120 Project UrbEx

17.08
Local youths had left their mark all over but nowhere as artfully as this pair of panties framed perfectly in sunlight. Party on!

17.09
The symmetry here is almost perfect, with nature adding taller saplings at the edges, shorter ones in the middle.

Asia

解説 N Amusement Park
Nara, Japan

When it opened in 1961, Nara Dreamland was the closest Japan had to Disneyland. It was even designed to look almost (but not quite) like a Disney resort, with a Main Street, a fairy-tale castle and even a huge wooden roller coaster – a very rare sight in this country.

But when Tokyo Disneyland opened in 1983, visitors preferred to go to that official park and Nara Dreamland attendance quickly dropped off. The park closed in 2006 after forty-five years and when I photographed it a few years later, it was shrouded in mist and parts of it were overgrown, although it was still a long way from falling apart and crumbling into dust.

Many Japanese people have happy memories of Nara Dreamland – it had 1.7 million visitors a year at the peak of its popularity – but I wasn't one of them. So I never got to have the experience of remembering it as the spotless, shiny, busy place I saw when I was a child, then re-exploring it in an abandoned state.

→p124

Project UrbEx

✕ Cultural/Entertainment
※ N Amusement Park
▣ Nara, Japan
▓ 2012

18.04

18.05

18.01 – 18.02
There is something uniquely spoooooky about empty theme parks. Is it because they are made for fun but now stand silent?

18.03 – 18.05
Nara Dreamland was modelled very closely on Disneyland in America – but I bet you had already guessed that!

18.06
The day I explored this site was so still and foggy, it seemed as though we were the only people left on the planet.

18.06

Asia 123

←p122

As an adult, I am far more interested in visiting closed theme parks, although since I am always also looking for thrills, I do go to the sort of places that have fast, screaming roller coasters. Be warned though – you will never, ever, see me in any cute theme park featuring big furry animals. Haha.

For a few years, this was a very well-known UrbEx destination, although after one explorer was sued by the management of Nara Dreamland for writing an article about visiting the site, UrbEx bloggers began to call it 'N Amusement Park' in print to avoid a similar fate.

And these days, it's completely gone. The demolition took a whole year between 2016 and 2017, so I think the site is now just an empty plot of weeds and concrete. I don't think it deserved to be torn down, but this often seems to be the fate of many abandoned places.

124   Project UrbEx

Asia

126 Project UrbEx

18.07 – 18.10
Askra, Screw Coaster, Bobsleigh and Fantasy Coaster – each very different roller coaster was inspired by famous rides built for theme parks around the world.

18.11 – 18.12
While part of Tommy's UrbEx mission has always been to record abandoned places, it's still hard to believe that this entire site was demolished in 2016.

Asia

解説 Wagakawa Plant
Iwate, Japan

I am very fond of huge concrete buildings and there are not many abandoned industrial sites in Japan on the scale of this 1940s hydropower plant up in the mountains, making it important to me. While I had expected everything to be big, I hadn't anticipated everything to be quite so vertical.

I have never been afraid of heights. I once had to stop climbing a radio tower in Europe because the ladder was missing in places. Another time, I was halfway up a chimney at an old Japanese coal mine when the ladder collapsed.

While I have always struggled to control my impulses, I must say that this place was the most difficult to find footholds. Every surface was concrete, so a fall would have turned me into a pancake. But I really wanted to get a picture of me on the big pipe, so I didn't hesitate. Let's go!

I used a rotten metal ladder to reach the central atrium, stretching my legs across the gap like a ninja. The inside of the pipe looked like thirty metres (100ft) straight down and there was only its narrow lip to balance on. ▶ And once I was there, I noticed another desperate threat lurking in this hopeless place. A hornet's nest close by. Shhh... stay quiet so as not to irritate the insects...

I am a person who acts as soon as I have an idea. That's dangerous, isn't it?

Project UrbEx

⚔ Industrial
※ Wagakawa Plant
▣ Iwate, Japan
▧ 2012

19.01
We had heard the walk in was difficult, but the river was so low that day, we crossed easily.

19.02 – 19.05
This must have looked huge in the 1940s, yet modern industrial buildings now dwarf it.

19.06
In a hydropower plant, the danger lies in every single pipe, conduit and access point leading down.

Asia

130　　　　　　　　　　Project UrbEx

19.07
How far down? Thirty metres (100ft) or more, I think. In my experience, trying not to think about falling is the best way to avoid doing so.

19.08
Not a split-screen view but a split-feed pipe, the shape designed to divert rushing water.

19.09
Even amid such huge, human-made towers of unbreakable concrete, little fragile pockets of nature will always find a way.

Asia   131

解説 Garbage Disposal Plant
Japan

In Japan, abandoned buildings of this scale are truly rare and I was amazed that such an incredibly enormous facility had ever been built for the sole purpose of incinerating garbage.

If I were a wealthy person, I would have purchased this place in 2013 and left it exactly as it was. The rusting steel, the huge machines, the smells and the atmosphere were great. I like industrial ruins best of all and although a friend visited this site a few years after I did, I fear that parts of it have since been demolished. Perhaps it's no longer there at all.

This plant was so big, it was hard to know where to start! A complex iron maze heading off to the left, right and all the way up. Wide pipes everywhere on every level, leading to giant valves and even more pipes. ▶ However many stairs we climbed, we could never see where we would end up. We got so tired going up and up, our legs started to tremble.

→p134

▶20.09

20.01

20.02

✕ Industrial
※ Garbage Disposal Plant
◉ Japan
▩ 2013

132　　　Project UrbEx

20.01
Infinite ceilings! The pipes and ladders vanished so far into the darkness that our legs ached from trying to climb so high.

20.02
Unimaginable capacity! This concrete hopper was built to hold trash from an entire city. Next to that, people looked like insects.

20.03
Endlessly long! If it were up to me, I would have bought this whole place and visited it daily. It really was the best!

20.04
Incredibly heavy! Compare the doors to the crossed concrete beams above them to appreciate the sheer mass of this place.

Asia

←p132
This was built to consume the garbage produced by an entire city, so nothing was on a human scale. We could trace the route the garbage took towards the incinerator, but the doors to the final areas were locked, so we couldn't enter.

I think it would have been a safe place for the workers when it was operating, but the fewer barriers that remain and the less safe it is, the more dynamic these abandoned spaces become. It was a thrilling moment to stand right on an unprotected edge and look down, down, down...

If I had fallen, I would have been one more piece of messy, wet trash on that vast concrete floor. While I sometimes feel like garbage about myself in my everyday life, nobody wants to end up like that, do they?

20.05
What a strange place to work. Watching an entire city's garbage pass by, all day, every day.

20.06
The safety barriers were damaged and even missing, leaving many dangerous – but thrilling – drops.

20.07 – 20.09
I heard it's all been demolished now... so sad. It should have become an UrbEx adventure zone.

134   Project UrbEx

Asia

解説 Ikeshima Island
Nagasaki, Japan

There's a Japanese proverb that says you can enjoy twice as much from only a single grain and Ikeshima Island is just that for UrbEx lovers. Only 4km in circumference, it's packed with a huge range of abandoned buildings, from industrial centres and apartment complexes ▶ to schools and even hot baths or 'onsen'. More like five times as much enjoyment from a single grain.

This island was a coal mine between 1959 and 2001 that, during its peak production, housed around eight thousand workers. It may look small on a map, but on the ground it actually feels vast and sprawling. There are so many steep slopes that it is difficult to get around without a car.

Despite being world famous for being an abandoned place, a declining number of locals – mostly retired miners – continue to live there. Yet the majority of the buildings are in an advanced state of disrepair, while facilities such as the hospital ▶ are so old and abandoned, they are no longer useful to the residents.

The wonderful thing about abandoned places in Japan is that they are rarely wrecked by visitors. This is probably a reflection of the thoughtful nature of the Japanese people, most of whom would never consider spraying graffiti on walls or smashing windows, even if they could get away with it.

→p138

▶ 21.09

21.01

▶ 21.06

21.02

21.03

Project UrbEx

21.01 – 21.03
Ikeshima is an UrbEx playground, with empty residential blocks, an industrial complex and overgrown landscapes in a very small area.

21.04
A control room frozen in time. Are the notes on the white board messages to the last ever shift who worked here?

21.05 – 21.06
It was hard to believe that decades had passed since the last patients were treated in this medical centre.

✕ Industrial/Domestic
※ Ikeshima Island
▣ Nagasaki, Japan
▧ 2020

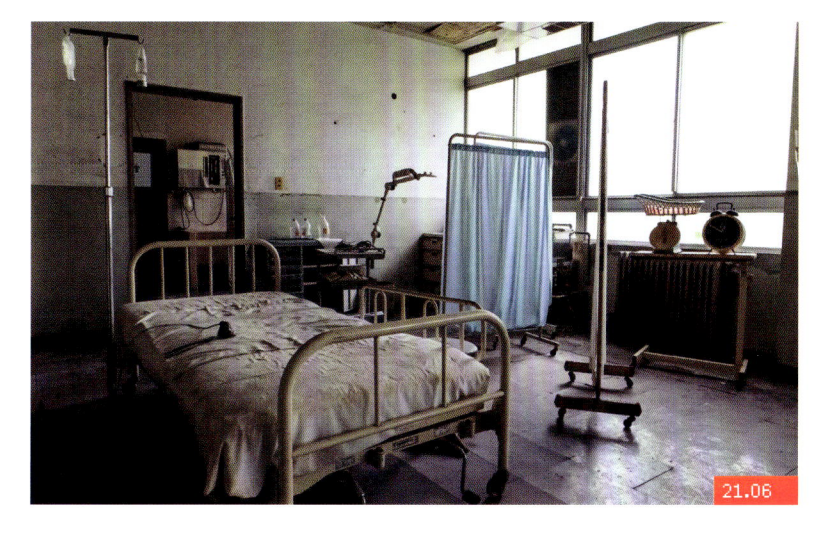

Asia   137

←p136

Of course, there are times when bad boys do mischief, with sad consequences. That is why we UrbExers can be so secretive about how we gain access to some places or even where they are – there's an entire section of 'secret places' at the end of this book. We Japanese explorers show respect to these places. We maintain the status quo, take only photographs and leave only footprints.

For that reason, I believe that Ikeshima Island will remain in this state of glorious decay. One hundred years from now, I can imagine that a visitor will see what I saw, only with more nature encroaching and the whole island perhaps becoming like Studio Ghibli's *Laputa*. Or perhaps some quirky foreign billionaire or company will buy the island and reuse it for an entirely new purpose. Who knows?

21.07 – 21.08
If several tonnes of metal fall at an abandoned industrial complex, do they make a sound?

21.09 – 21.10
You could explore here for weeks and still not see every room. Imagine what secrets lie inside.

21.11
Incredibly, a few people – mostly retired workers – still lived on the island, surrounded by silence.

138   Project UrbEx

Asia

Project UrbEx

Asia 141

解説 Niigata Russian Village
Niigata, Japan

The Russian Village opened in 1993 as a cultural exchange theme park but since it was never very popular, it closed in 2004. The nearby Turkish Village in Kashiwazaki also shut down and there was even an old Wild West theme park near Kinugawa Onsen (Japanese people must have briefly been excited by cowboys for a few years).

All have left a lot of exhibits to see, such as the Russian Village's Mammoth Illusion Studio and Suzdal Church. They also pose the interesting question: 'Why did they build so many foreign village theme parks in Japan?'

Since Japan is an island nation, it has a habit of yearning for other countries. There are German village theme parks still operating here, along with Spanish, Dutch and many other European-themed tourist destinations. In Hokkaido, Gluck Kingdom was based on medieval Germany, although that, too, is now abandoned.

When Japan was in its successful bubble economy in the 1980s, many such parks were built, yet few survived after the bubble burst in 1991. This has left UrbExers many ruins to explore. I now love how the thematic outer skins of each one peels away to reveal the exact same plain concrete foundations. The fact that they are so superficial and fake is a major appeal to me.

▶ 22.02

▶ 22.03

22.01

22.02

142 Project UrbEx

22.01 – 22.02
The superficiality of theme parks fascinates me, especially when time and the elements strip away the veneer to reveal concrete.

22.03 – 22.04
There's very little Russian about the frames of these buildings. The red one could be a hardware superstore, for instance.

22.05
It's often only inside abandoned theme parks that all the little details added by the original designers survive.

✕ Cultural/Entertainment
※ Niigata Russian Village
▣ Niigata, Japan
※ 2013

Asia 143

22.06 – 22.08
Concrete always returns to being flat and grey, while nature will march across human-made spaces. All it takes is time.

22.09 – 22.11
To Japanese visitors, the lure of such a foreign destination wasn't enough for this place to survive more than a few years.

144 Project UrbEx

22.09

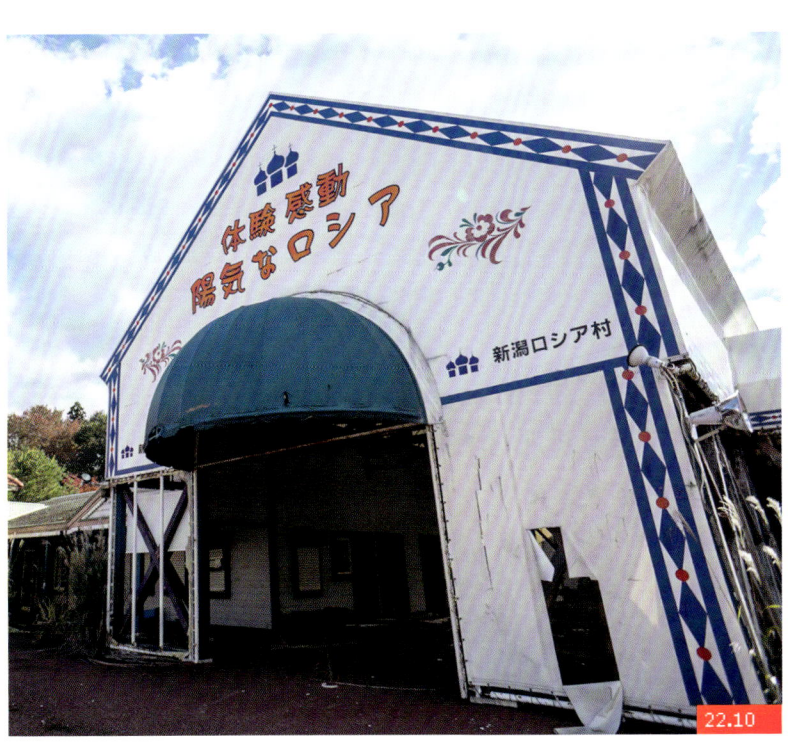

22.10

22.11

Asia

✕ Tourism
※ Bedugul Taman Hotel
▣ Bali, Indonesia
▩ 2020

23.01 – 23.02
Built into a hillside, the hotel steps down the slopes in a series of terraces, mirroring the farmed land on the surrounding peaks.

23.03 – 23.05
The abandoned hotel has become a tourist destination, resulting in the locals maintaining it in a clean and tidy state of decay.

146 Project UrbEx

解說 Bedugul Taman Hotel
Bali, Indonesia

I am an urban explorer, but I am also a ghost hunter. I love buildings with the kind of history that helps to create horror games, so Bali's 'Ghost Palace' was a treat. While I know it was built in the 1990s and closed in the 2000s, all the other details changed depending on who I spoke to.

One local told me, 'A political faction was staying at the hotel, but all of them disappeared overnight.' But I was also told, 'A bunch of corrupt politicians were executed here.' Other theories involve the ghosts of construction workers and links to the family of Indonesia's President Suharto. Many Balinese places have dark histories.

It seems most likely that the tourist downturn after the 2002 Bali bombing sealed the fate of the hotel, which has now become a tourist attraction on its own. Inside, I could sense some of its former atmosphere. There was little destruction, and the locals had kept it neat and tidy. Some now even charge visitors an entrance fee!

▶23.06

The hotel, perched on the edge of a cliff,▶ remains a spectacular sight. It's surrounded by terraced fields and also has levels stepping down the hillside. I'm not surprised it continues to attract tourists as well as UrbExers.

23.03

23.04

23.05

Asia   147

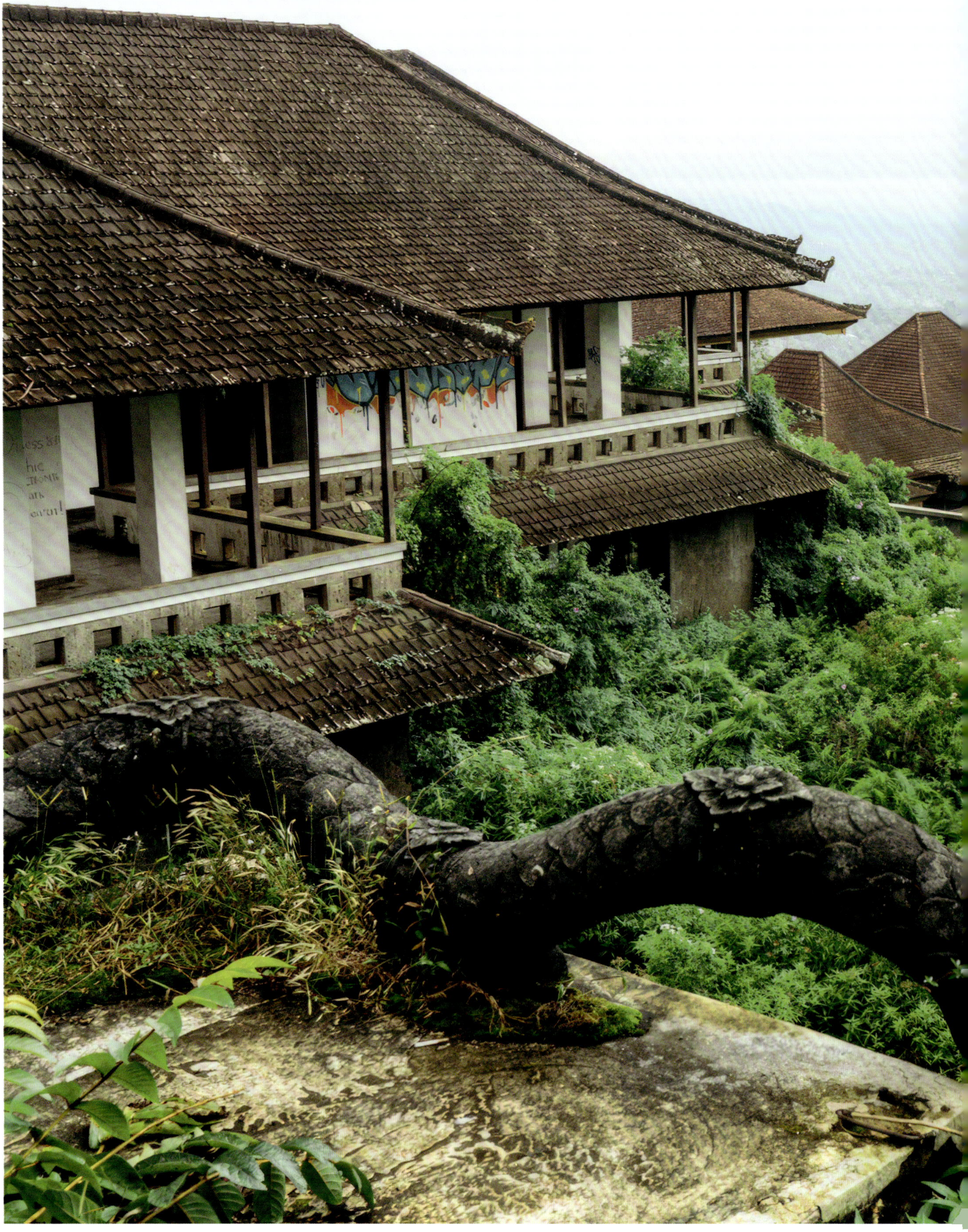

Asia 149

150   Project UrbEx

23.06 – 23.08
Once a favourite hotel of rich businessmen and politicians, the dragon statues still give the place a certain 'place of power' vibe.

23.09 – 23.10
With so many staring eyes, is it any surprise that the hotel now has a reputation as being a haunted or cursed place?

Asia

151

解説 Houtouwan Fishing Village
Shengshan Island, China

Shengshan Island in the east of China is a popular holiday destination for Chinese tourists, with many also taking a day trip up to the north of the island in order to visit Houtouwan – the famous deserted fishing village.

As you must have realized, I rarely travel to popular destinations so that I can buy souvenirs from tourist resort shops, so when I took the boat trip to Shengshan Island in 2015, my mission was to bypass the busy holiday spots and head straight for the village. This involved a super-wild ride on a motorcycle taxi, which was an adventure all of its own, not least because the road was very rough, and the taxi was loaded up with gas cans.

The village is not an ancient one and was built in the 1950s as part of a planned fisheries development. For a while, over two thousand people lived there in hundreds of homes. Life was good. But over time, the villagers realized they were living a hard life with few amenities compared to their neighbours. From the 1990s onwards, most left in search of a better life. Not everyone went, though. Since a few families remained – and are still there ▶ – Houtouwan isn't quite a true ghost town.

→p156

▶24.13

24.01

24.02

24.03

✕ Domestic
※ Houtouwan Fishing Village
▣ Shengshan Island, China
▩ 2015

24.01 – 24.03
Built as a single, planned project in the 1950s to support a growing fishing industry, Houtouwan must have been a fine place to live…

24.04 – 24.06
…if you had strong legs and didn't mind walking up and down hills. Without roads, everything must have been carried too.

152 Project UrbEx

Asia

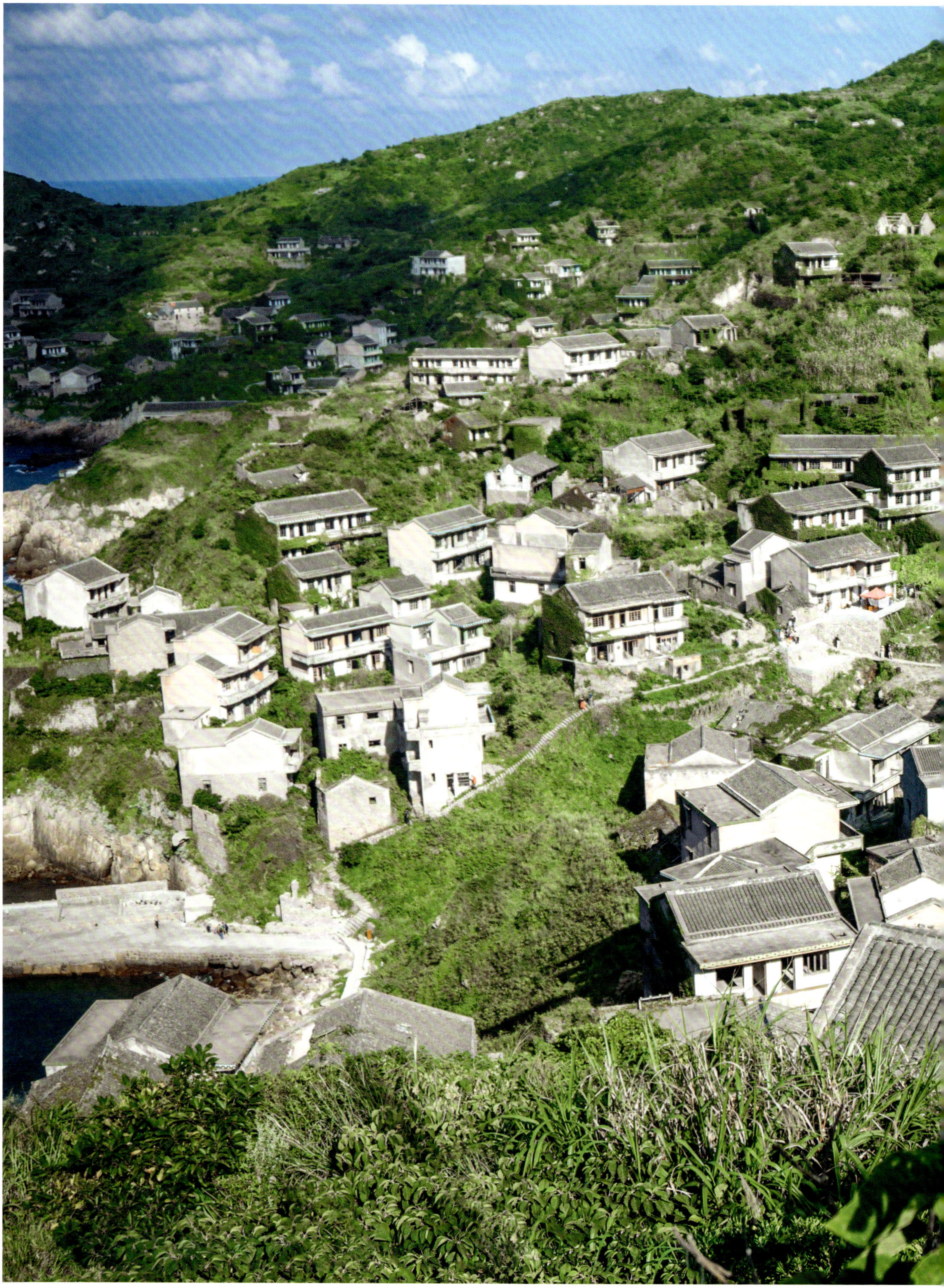

Asia

←p152
Many small villages have been abandoned around the world, but few become popular tourist sites. One reason for Houtouwan's continuing popularity is the complex way that the stone buildings are arranged up and down the hillside. Due to this, visitors used to think they had strayed into a mysterious world. Chinese visitors refer to it by a name that translates as 'A Village of Fairy Tale'. Maybe Japanese visitors should scream 'Laputa!!!'

But the main reason tourists come here must be the vegetation. It's not unusual for abandoned places to become overgrown, but few get as swallowed up as the fishing village. Ivy has covered many of the buildings so tightly, they seem to have been deliberately wrapped in greenery. What a strange and unusual sight.

Project UrbEx

24.07 – 24.09
The vegetation coating many of the buildings is all so uniformly green that it seems deliberate, not nature taking over.

24.10 – 24.11
Despite the scenic location, the village gradually depopulated as people tired of a life offering only the basic essentials.

Asia

157

24.12
An abandoned place? Not quite. When I visited, a few villagers – and their dogs – still had their homes in-between the ruins.

24.13
The modern world seems to have passed by Houtouwan, with little in the way of amenities and not even running water.

24.14
It's very Instagrammable though, right? No wonder so many Chinese tourists take the day trip to get memorable selfies.

Project UrbEx

Asia

解説 Gunkanjima
Nagasaki, Japan

Gunkanjima is the rock star of abandoned places – a destination so famous that even people who don't know what UrbEx is have heard of it. I first went there in 2007… then just kept returning.

▶ 25.01

Hashima Island – its name on the maps – looks like a giant warship, ▶ hence its nickname '*Gunkan-Jima*' or 'Battleship Island'. Undersea coal mines surfaced here and, from the 1880s onwards, mining waste enlarged the island until a vast concrete sea wall was built to protect it, making it ship-shaped. By the 1950s, over five thousand workers lived on it and worked under it. Then, when the coal ran out in the 1970s, it was abandoned quickly, leaving many fascinating personal objects behind. ▶

▶ 25.14

Every time I approach the island by boat, my heart feels ready to burst out of my mouth. On my first visit in 2007, I went straight to the Hashima Shrine and prayed to the Gunkanjima god for my safe exploration. The island's lonely atmosphere, concrete buildings and narrow walkways left me speechless, and I have never recovered. No matter how hard I try, I can never describe my impression of this place using words. Instead, I try to make my photos show my awe.

My second landing was in 2008, roaming the island with four other women and realizing I would have to keep returning. I could have stayed for days but was only there for a few blissful hours.
→p162

25.01
Battleship Island is deservedly one of the world's most famous UrbEx destinations. Every time I approach it, my pulse quickens.

25.02
It's such a small space – about 400 metres (1,300ft) long, under 150 metres (500ft) wide – yet, in the 1950s, over five thousand workers lived here.

25.03
Search on YouTube and you can find black-and-white photos and films of the island. It must have been so noisy and cramped.

⚒ Industrial/Domestic
※ Gunkanjima
🏠 Nagasaki, Japan
🎞 2007, 2013, 2022

25.01

Project UrbEx

25.02

25.03

Asia

162 Project UrbEx

←p160

By 2010, wider perceptions of the island had changed, it was now being recognized as an established tourist destination, and about half of the island had been opened for sightseeing.

Since I was now able to stay longer and explore more, I could see what a national treasure it was and that the whole place deserved to be protected for future generations. And that's exactly what happened later, in 2015, when it became a UNESCO World Heritage Site.

I kept going back, returning with different friends in both 2011 and 2012. And then, in 2013, my group finally got to spend a full day and night on the island. This meant that when the evening came, the apartment we had chosen as our base camp was illuminated by the lovely light of the setting sun. Simply beautiful!

25.04
The island was attracting so many visitors that in 2015, it was made UNESCO World Heritage Site, guaranteeing its preservation.

164 Project UrbEx

25.05
The buildings on the island are some of Japan's first reinforced concrete constructions, built to protect workers from typhoons.

25.06 – 25.08
Single workers lived in shared dorm rooms, but there were also families here. Imagine being a child growing up here!

Asia

165

Project UrbEx

Asia

25.09
The lack of light pollution made the night sky crystal clear.

25.10 – 25.11
The first accommodation blocks were built in 1916 and life must have been very boring and basic at the start – just work and sleep.

25.12 – 25.13
As more workers came here, everything from a cinema and school, to gardens and a pachinko parlour were built.

Project UrbEx

25.11

25.12

25.13

Asia 169

170 Project UrbEx

25.14 – 25.15
The mine closed in 1974, creating a time capsule from everything left behind. The child who played here would now be over 50.

25.16
Would life have been good here? Maybe not, although it might have been comfortable by the end of the mine's life.

25.17 – 25.18
Say 'Ahhhh!' With so many people and a coal mine on such a tiny island, medical and dental dramas must have happened every day.

Asia 171

26.01
Ever wondered what the early stages of a zombie apocalypse would look like? Me too. This place answered a lot of questions.

26.02 – 26.03
This was once the biggest hotel in the country – a Japanese Palace of Versailles cast in concrete for paying customers.

172 Project UrbEx

解説 Hachijo Oriental Resort
Izu Islands, Japan

The door was held shut by a sickle lodged through the handles. An actual Grim Reaper curved blade… it was very foreboding. I peeked through a window and saw hanging laundry and some piles of recent refuse. It was hard not to ask myself, 'Is someone living here? And are they an active, sickle-wielding serial killer?'

Hachijo Oriental Resort is one of those places that stood still as the world around it changed. It's on Hachijo-jima ('*jima*' is a Japanese suffix meaning 'island') nearly 300km south of Tokyo. It's such a remote place that it was where political enemies were exiled in the 17th, 18th and 19th centuries. It was also the site of a secret submarine base during the Second World War.

In the years after the war it became known as the 'Hawaii of Japan', and in 1963 Japan's largest hotel was built. Originally called The Royal Hotel, this was remodelled as Pricia Resort Hachijo in the 1990s and then reopened again as The Hachijo Oriental Resort in the early 2000s. ▶ But by then, Japanese tourists had decided they preferred the actual Hawaii to the Hawaii of Japan and with fewer guests every year, the hotel closed in 2006.

I went there shortly afterwards, in 2014, and it was fascinating to witness the early stages of abandonment. It was a truly huge complex, with an overwhelming facade looking like a Japanese Palace of Versailles. Hard to believe that such a great building was no longer used by anyone.

Going inside – although avoiding the serial killer's lair – most of the rooms were so clean and tidy that they could have been dusted off and put back into service. ▶ The foyer areas retained their luxurious furniture, while it was only the guest rooms with open windows that had started to rot. ▶ Yet even these looked really cool, I thought.

▶ 26.01

▶ 26.07

▶ 26.08

26.01

26.03

✈ Tourism
※ Hachijo Oriental Resort
◉ Izu Islands, Japan
▓ 2014

Asia 173

26.04 – 26.05
Eight years of abandonment had barely affected the hotel's exterior, apart from the foliage...

26.06
...but inside, the impact depended on how sealed an area was. From the room with a window open...

26.07
...to an immaculate, tidy and dry suite that you could have stayed in. Even the curtains were clean...

26.08
...which is more than could be said for this room, battered by the seasons and soaked by the rain.

Project UrbEx

26.06

26.07

26.08

Asia

✈ Cultural/Entertainment
※ Hokkaido Sex Museum
◉ Jozankei Onsen, Japan
▨ 2014

176　　　Project UrbEx

解説

Hokkaido Sex Museum
Jozankei Onsen, Japan

To my generation, places like this are nearly extinct, making the few that remain of great value. It seems that in the 1970s and 1980s, there was at least one sex museum in every tourist destination in Japan. My father and mother tell me that they visited one when they were young, so I suppose that visitors either went to laugh at the exhibits, or they dared each other to be naughty and see what was inside.

This museum was in a rather lonely part of the tourist area, with only a few restaurants and residences in the neighbourhood. The exterior was eerie, but the impact of a huge Buddha standing forlornly was amazing. ▶The doors stood open forever, in the spirit of free love and sex. I walked in just as any other tourist would have in the past.

The Hokkaido sex museum opened in 1980 in a flurry of excitement but the building was very run down by 2007, and it closed for good in 2010. The first room was so dark, I turned on the flashlight and saw a life-sized model of a whale's sexual organs... speechless. There was a terrible smell, which I quickly found was coming off a rotting snake that had fallen out of a broken bottle.

I passed a very... powerful... statue of a stallion in the second room and entered the largest exhibition space, which was reminiscent of a 1980s Japanese strip bar. The two mechanical target games were strange but amazing. In the first (my favourite), tourists would have squirted a slimy liquid in the direction of an 'open legs Egyptian woman'.
→p179

▶27.01

27.01 – 27.02
From the outside, nothing screams 'sex museum'. Perhaps that was the appeal – the thrill of hidden secrets within.

27.03 – 27.04
Indeed, the cafe looks just like any other cafe. Although maybe, to most visitors, food and sex were an uncomfortable pairing.

27.04

Asia

27.05
Inside, in windowless rooms away from the prying eyes of the public on the street, things rapidly got stranger.

27.06
Bottoms up! It seems that these cancan dancers with winking rear-ends were once rigged to mechanically wiggle and jiggle.

27.07 – 27.09
The darker the room, the more the sex museum lived up to its name. Imagine all the visitors who must have laughed nervously here.

178 Project UrbEx

←p177
The second game – French Pon Pon – encouraged players to wait until a series of cancan dancer dolls raised their skirts. A French cancan shooter. Wow! That's FPS! After that, the wild animal orgy in the final room seemed quite tame. Was this display of *National Geographic Wild* meant to represent the power of nature?

It's just my opinion, but I think this type of odd museum must be a part of Japanese culture that feeds a national interest in scary things and fringe-artistic, boundary pushing expression. The Japanese people, myself included, have a '*hentai*' spirit in our hearts. But in a good way.

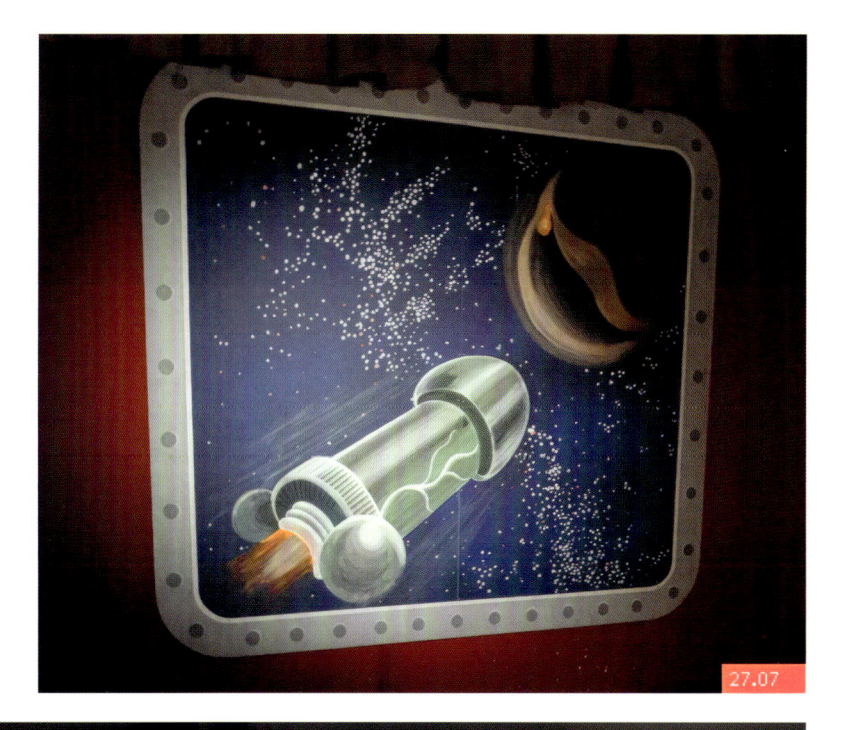

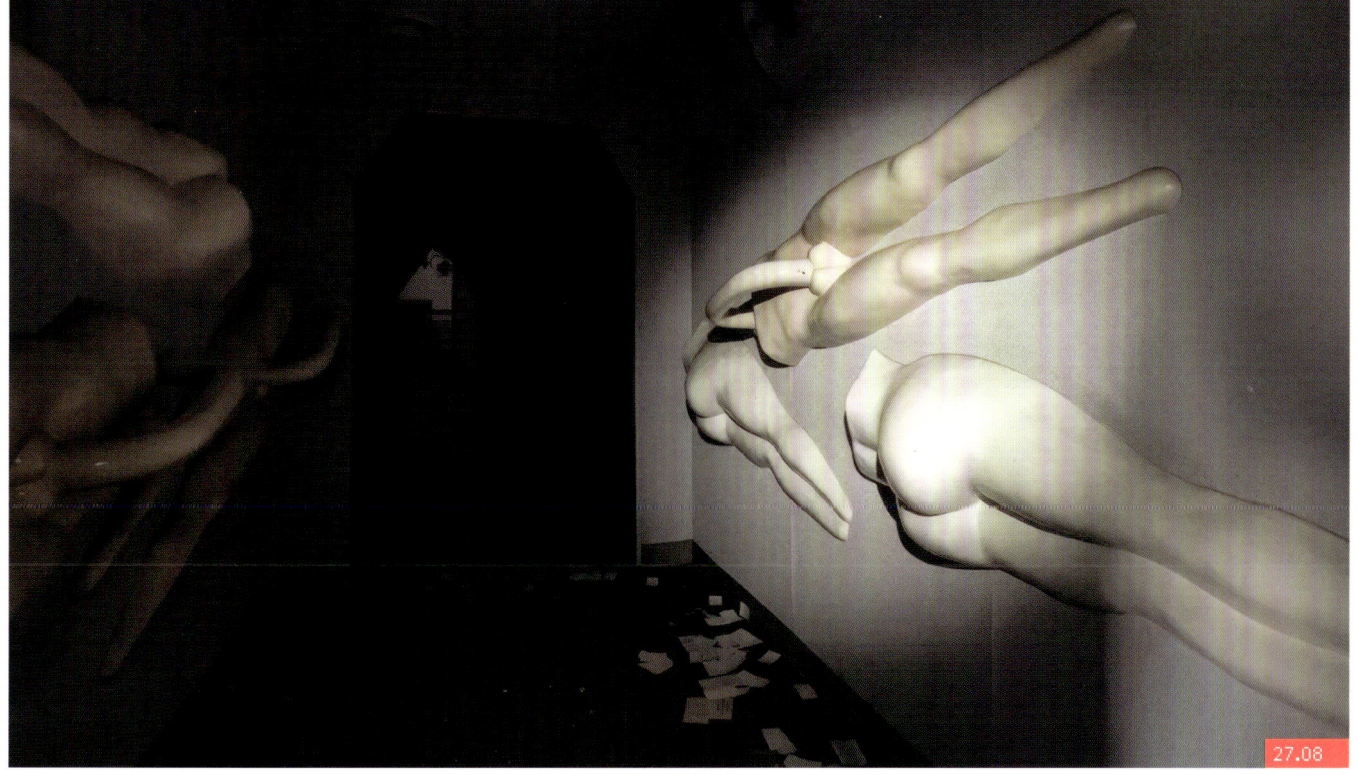

Asia 179

Lumber Processing Plant, p190

● Location Classified
● 28-33

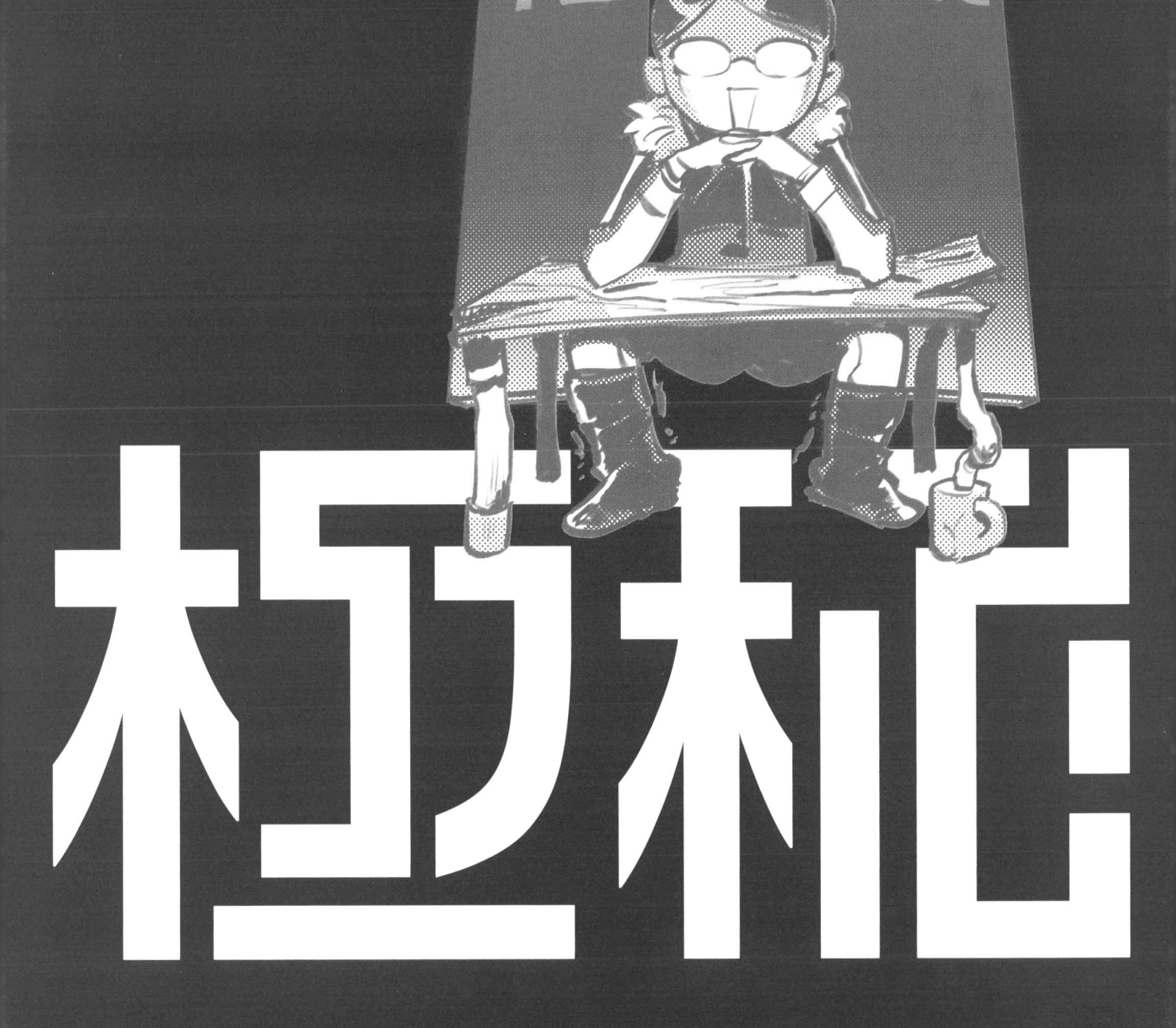

✂ Domestic
※ An Abandoned Villa
▣ Europe
▧ 2014

28.01
Abandoned or just currently unoccupied? Much of the house seemed mothballed but complete.

28.02
Many of the once 'modern' conveniences bought since the 1920s now show their age.

28.03 – 28.05
A family grew up and then grew old in this house, leaving a record of every stage of their lives.

182　　　Project UrbEx

解説 An Abandoned Villa
A quiet suburb, Europe

I loved walking around this house, but I also got the slightly uneasy feeling that it hadn't been quite abandoned by its owner. Because of this, I was very careful to leave everything in its place and I am unwilling to fully divulge its location.

From the outside, it doesn't look deserted at all. I was told that a rich lawyer and his family had owned it since the 1920s but that when first he died, followed by his wife a few years later, the children hadn't wanted to move in. Since they hadn't wanted to sell it either, the house was left to rot over the years.

Each slowly decaying room was so full of possessions and unique characteristics ▶ that my tour became like a detective mystery, with clues everywhere that told me more and more about the habits of the family who used to live there.

→p185

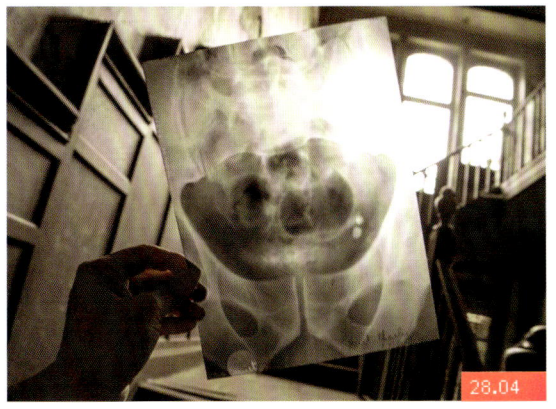

▶28.07

Location Classified

184　　Project UrbEx

←p183
I learned from all the religious objects that someone had been a pious Christian. I was then surprised to see live shotgun cartridges spilling out of a box, although did that also explain why there was a stuffed raven on display, forever flapping angrily above an empty fireplace?

Food still on kitchen shelves, magazines ready to read on a bedroom floor and computers looking decades out of date – had anything at all ever been removed from this house?

Then, in the basement, past walls where children had once scribbled drawings, the final treasures – a wine cellar and shelves upon shelves of legal documents. Here, I could see what sort of person one of the owners had been – an organized man who left his affairs in order, as neat and tidy as a library.

The cold and damp may have made the shelves sag, the paper peel and the paint flake, but it would be many more years before they erased this sense of efficiency.

28.06 – 28.07
A sink pulled away from the wall and light fittings gradually rotated upside-down on mildew-covered walls as time passed slowly in the abandoned villa.

28.08 – 28.09
The amount of personal photos offered what seemed to be a complete family record stretching across most of the 20th century.

28.10
The random nature of decay, with the left of the room almost pristine but the right side water damaged and rotting.

Location Classified

185

28.11

28.12

186   Project UrbEx

28.11 – 28.12
More decay randomness, with one room all but destroyed yet the 1970s preserved in another.

28.13
Is this how the kitchen shelves were stocked on the day the final occupant of this house died?

28.14
Holiday snapshots and postcards spanning different continents and post-war decades.

28.15
Enough live shotgun shells to start a small war, even if it's only against the local crows.

Location Classified

188   Project UrbEx

28.16 – 28.17
Thousands of records carefully and neatly filed away. But do they even matter any more? Will they ever be read again?

28.18 – 28.19
Has this wine soured into vinegar or matured into magnificence? And will anyone ever uncork a bottle to find out?

Location Classified

29.01 – 29.02
Nature always takes over when a place is abandoned and in jungles, the speed of change is incredible. Trees seem to grow overnight!

29.03 – 29.04
The facility was so large and full of heavy machinery that it must have been incredibly noisy when in operation. Not quiet, like now.

解説 # Lumber Processing Plant
Deep in the jungle, Asia

CRACK! I stopped slapping at giant mosquitoes and jumped in surprise as a branch snapped and a troop of startled monkeys suddenly ran away from us through the trees. I wanted to watch them but my friend told me not to look at them directly, since a stare might make them turn around and attack us.

When I go to cold places, I often carry a whistle to repel bears. Since this was a jungle, I'd come here with chemical repellent spray to keep the insects away, even though it did nothing to protect me from these monster bugs. I hadn't even thought about packing something to save me from a violent monkey rampage, though.

The road through the mountainous jungle had been well-maintained, and I remember waving to active-looking surveillance cameras on the way in. Yet the interior of this lumber plant looked totally abandoned, and it was being swallowed up by the jungle in record time. ▶The warehouses were massive, with the red cypress trees that had once been cut down and processed here greedily rooting and taking over. Revenge!
→p194

▶29.12

29.01

29.02

190　　　　Project UrbEx

✘ Industrial
※ Lumber Processing Plant
◉ Asia
▦ 2017

Location Classified

29.05

29.06

29.07

192　　　　　　　　　　Project UrbEx

29.05 – 29.06
An intact lab in the middle of the jungle was a rare and crazy sight. Most bottles contained unknown substances I dared not touch.

29.07 – 29.09
A jungle environment is always hard on human-made structures, with rust, rot and erosion taking place at an accelerated pace.

Location Classified

←p190

A faded site map on the wall of some kind of laboratory showed us how huge this entire facility had once been. So few people had visited since its closure that the contents of the lab were intact and untouched on the shelves – everything from medicinal substances to specialist supplies with faded labels in Japanese. I don't see that level of preservation very often on my adventures.

Back out in the warehouse, the overhead sunlight was beaming down through the holes in the roof into the giant, wild, botanical garden that had grown out of the floor. I could hear the sound of birds chirping, frogs singing and water dripping. It was the world of *The Last of Us*... only with millions of killer mosquitoes.

29.10

29.11

Project UrbEx

29.10 – 29.12
Three different storage areas demonstrated the stages of natural encroachment, from no plants to a complete rainforest.

Location Classified

解説 The Empty City
An industrial zone, Asia

Protected by a very old security guard and one stray dog, this empty city still stands tall but silent. When the two of them heard that we were explorers from Japan, they both graciously let us onto the property. I often come across such kindness, and I am grateful to all the kind people I have encountered.

These accommodation blocks used to stand next to a huge factory and they were home to the majority of its employees, as well as their families. Even though everything was built from bare concrete, I still found it harsh but beautiful. The complex looked more like a military fortress than housing (it would be called a '*danchi*' in Japanese), but I loved the sight of multiple buildings of the same form repeating off into the distance. ▶

These lines of concrete building standing on open land created an unreal, lonely mood. It was clear that many, many people used to live here at one time, which makes it a little sad that so little human life was left behind in this empty place. The only signs of life were the street lamps ▶ with their untidy bundles of electric wiring spilling out.

This empty city was very atmospheric – a perfect example of a lonely, abandoned place.

▶ 30.06

▶ 30.05

30.01

30.02

30.03

✵ Industrial/Domestic
※ The Empty City
▣ Asia
▦ 2017

30.01
Like a military base, a fortress or a videogame level, the different levels and rooftops just seemed to offer sight lines and defences.

30.02 – 30.04
With balconies, steps and porches all cast in concrete, this empty city looks ready to stand the test of time and outlive us all.

30.05
Where workers once headed to the nearby factories, the only thing marching down this street now is nature.

196　　　　　Project UrbEx

Location Classified

30.06
One design repeated in rough concrete produced an unreal pattern. Digital cut-and-paste displayed in an analogue world.

Location Classified

30.07 – 30.08
Stripped of their furnishings, paintings and, of course, their people, the empty city's family homes all looked like bunkers.

30.09 – 30.10
It took a lot of imagination to think of these places full of life and laughter, colour and noise, since they were so still, grey and quiet.

Project UrbEx

Location Classified 201

解說 UFO Houses
A stormy beach, Asia

The aliens must have thought they had grabbed a good spot when they claimed this beach as their vacation resort in the late 1970s. But in true sci-fi movie style, Planet Earth's climate stopped the invasion far better than any military intervention. Originally a resort of almost a hundred structures, and with many more planned, only a few UFO-shaped pods ▸ remained when I visited and even then, their future was in doubt.

▸ 31.02

A local property developer built these chalets – modelled on the 1960s European 'Futuro' design – as a high-class holiday resort for travellers and the ultra-rich, but the project seemed doomed to fail from the very start.

A lack of funding plagued construction throughout 1978, as did superstitious fears surrounding the nearby graveyard. Also, everyone quickly realized that this beach would never be a good vacation spot. The region is ridiculously hot in the summer, while winter storms cause high tides that constantly smash a combination of sea water and sand into the pods. ▸

▸ 31.10

→p204

202 Project UrbEx

⊗ Domestic
※ UFO Houses
◎ Asia
▦ 2017

31.01
This holiday complex was planned as a mix of different shapes and designs, from individual boxes to box towers and UFOs.

31.02 – 31.03
These UFOs are based on the 'Futuro Pod', a prefabricated house designed in the 1960s by Finnish architect Matti Suuronen.

Location Classified

←p202

The resort was closed in 1980 and when I visited, the few remaining UFO houses were boarded up and surrounded by barbed wire. Each circular UFO is a fibreglass shell that houses a spacious kitchen, bedroom and bathroom. I spotted one room with '*tatami*' mats, so I guess they were hoping to welcome Japanese tourists.

But when I climbed in, everything smelled of mould, while the crazy heat hit me immediately. Outside, the temperature was exceeding 42°C – far too scorching to sit on the beach. Inside this alien's UFO, it wasn't only hot enough to mutilate cattle, you could have cooked them too!

I'm convinced it was this summer heat trapped inside these closed pods that doomed the resort, not the nearby graveyard overlooking the sea. But since I love urban legends, a spooky story about why this place closed is more romantic and fascinating than one about a local businessman and his failed tourist resort venture.

31.04 – 31.05
On a beach where the summertime heat exceeds 40°C, these poorly ventilated and insulated pods were very uncomfortable places.

Location Classified

Project UrbEx

Location Classified 207

31.06 – 31.08
It seemed that while the vision and concept were great, the location and the execution of these holiday homes were flawed.

31.09 – 31.10
The devastating power of the winter storms and high tides was clear to see. Even if developers don't clear this site, the sea will.

208 Project UrbEx

Random Observations on Global Urban Exploration #4

Project UrbEx

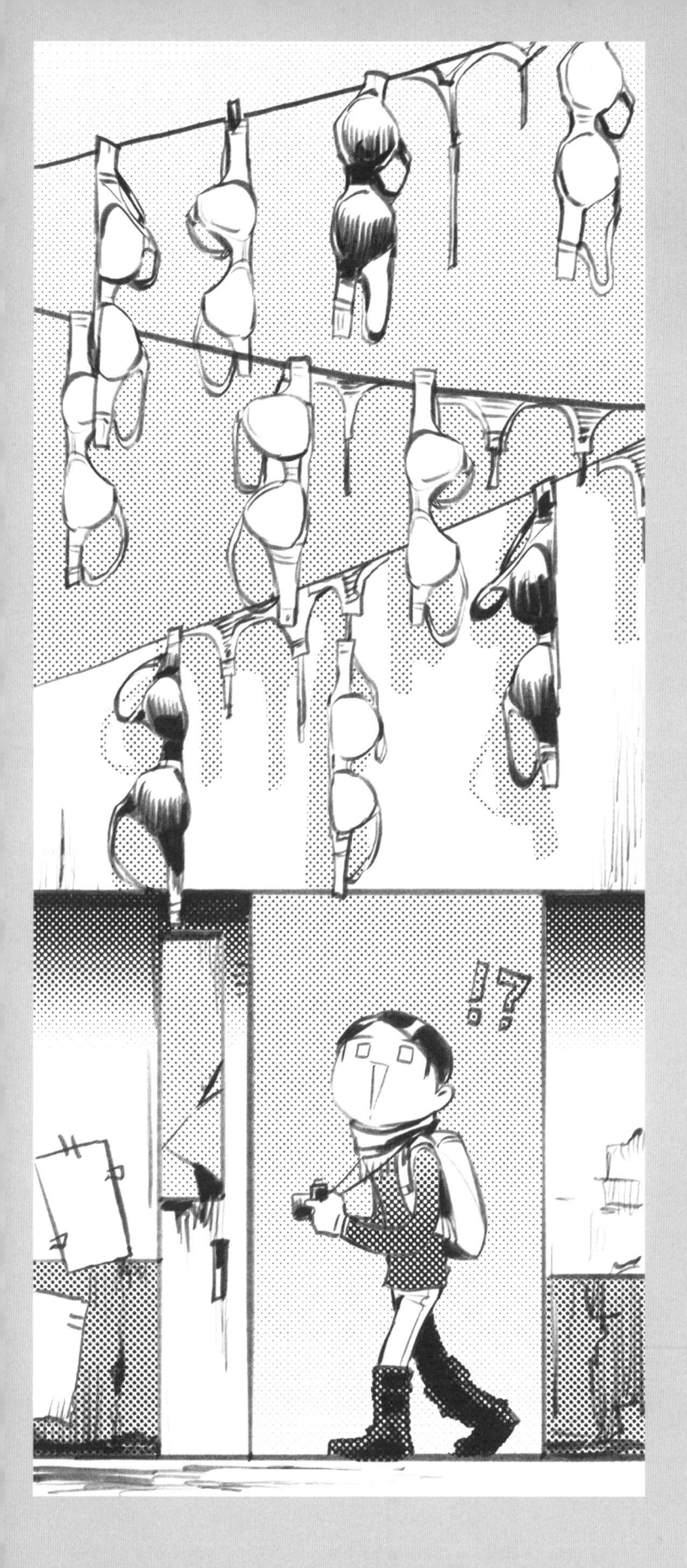

'A bra temple is always going to be a bizarre and confusing place'

I've already written about the 'strange cult's bra temple' elsewhere in this book, so you can go and look at the photographs I took on p210. But a bra temple is such a weird and slightly disturbing place that I can't get it out of my head. And I think it should live inside your imagination, too!

Let's just go over the facts again. Every bra in the temple was the same cup size. Many were attached to the walls with garter belts. The name of one woman had been printed out many times onto sheets of paper that were then pinned to the walls and attached to... you guessed it... bras.

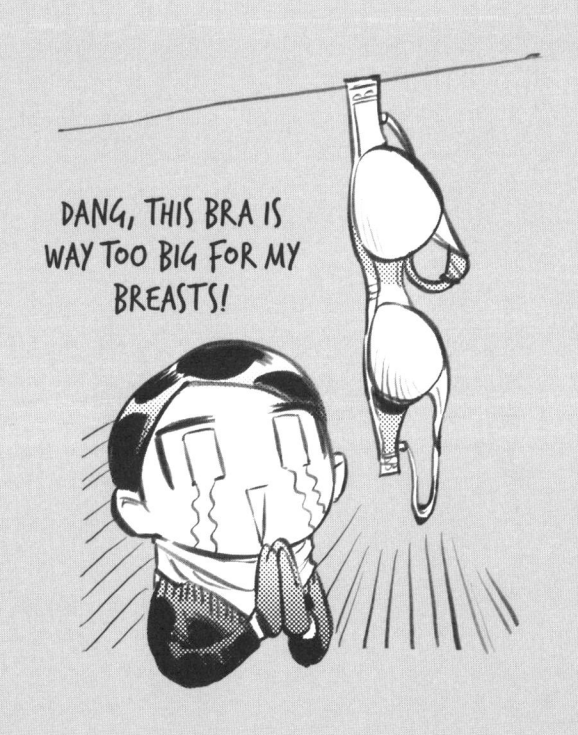

DANG, THIS BRA IS WAY TOO BIG FOR MY BREASTS!

Random Observations

Project UrbEx

'Understand the risks of urban exploration, but don't fear them'

Is creeping around abandoned buildings dangerous? Well, yes, of course it has risks. But having a sense of self-preservation by staying alert keeps you safe... most of the time. There are many physical dangers in crumbling buildings that have been locked up for years, or even decades – heights, toxic dust, rotten floors and equally rotten animals. Bits of walls and ceilings often just drop right off... it can be very startling!

Water inside empty buildings is a real red flag, since it can hide hazards like holes or sharp metal. Also, is the water in a flooded basement clear because it's clean, or because it is so polluted with acid or chemicals that nothing living can grow in it?

While some explorers might take calculated risks in certain situations, entering still and dark water without proper equipment or knowledge of the conditions is generally discouraged. The risks associated with contaminated water are so significant that I usually think it's safer to retreat and find alternative routes.

UrbEx is very much like any other activity, if you think it looks dangerous, it's probably dangerous. What you do about it is up to you.

Random Observations

I'm never going to jump out and Solid Snake someone for just doing their job, of course, but hiding in the shadows, listening out for approaching footsteps and seeing flashlight beams bouncing off the walls can make the thrill of exploration that extra bit exciting.

Project UrbEx

'It's all a game'

I love videogames, of course. They are what I think about during my days, what I dream about at night and, of course, what I have spent my career helping to create. So while it is natural that I seek out game-like experiences in all aspects of my life, I also think it's not strange that I turn real-world experiences into games.

And what could be more game-like than exploration? Finding a way in – and out – is core to many videogames, just as solving puzzles and discovering treasures are. But nothing gets my little heart beating quite as quickly as real-world escape and evasion.

Don't get me wrong, I don't actively go looking to tangle with security guards or avoid regular patrols. But when I do, it really is very, very exciting!

Level completed, achievement unlocked, power-ups awarded – these are all game concepts that are easy to bring over into the real-world and even your everyday life. I say that you've gotta keep aiming for those high scores, because when it's game over in life, it really is game over.

Random Observations

'While I pass through these places, other people live there'

Deserts and jungles look like alien planets to me, yet I have to remind myself that these distant, exotic locations are places that are just around the corner to the local people. I remembered this as I walked through an abandoned flight school in the former East Germany, originally built by the Nazis, but in fact used mainly by Soviet airmen.

Yet all this history was of no concern to the old man blocking my access as he happily sunbathed in the yard outside the building – completely naked! To me, this old school was a piece of history in a German suburb. To him, it was a quiet spot for relaxation and refreshment.

Project UrbEx

Location Classified

32.01
Looks harmless enough, right? But anyone thinking this exterior houses something innocent would be so very, very wrong.

32.02
Stairway to... insanity? Visitors with an extreme sensitivity to underwear, or a phobia of bras, should turn back now...

32.03 – 32.05
...because the more you explore this cult's bizarre temple, the further and further down the rabbit hole you get.

Project UrbEx

解説 Strange Cult's Bra Temple
In the mountains, Asia

Is this an art installation, a shrine to underwear or just the strangest monument to a relationship break-up ever created? I have been exploring abandoned places for many years, but this site that I visited in 2016 was one of the creepiest. So many questions! So few answers!!!

I can't even say for sure that this was an abandoned place. This person – let's call them 'The Author' – had left a stack of questionnaires for visitors to complete. They also seemed to be returning regularly to update their masterpiece.

Art? Maybe. Bra temple? Definitely. Has one person ever been surrounded by more bras? Surprisingly, every one – most of them attached to the walls by garter belts ▶ – was exactly the same cup size. That's psychotic.

The Author seemed to hold a fascination for that bra size as well as a grudge against a certain woman, whose name appeared on photocopied sheets pinned everywhere. ▶ As terrifying as it was to imagine a man being this angry or obsessed about a woman to create this, I also remember shivers running down my spine when I realized The Author might be female. A woman's grudge is so frightening, you see…

This place is also home to the Japanese cult group I named 'Fraud Temple' on my blog, since it seems to have conned many highly educated people. The bra temple is part of a cult industry then. It's one of the strangest places I have ever visited. Also, not one I'd recommend to tourists.

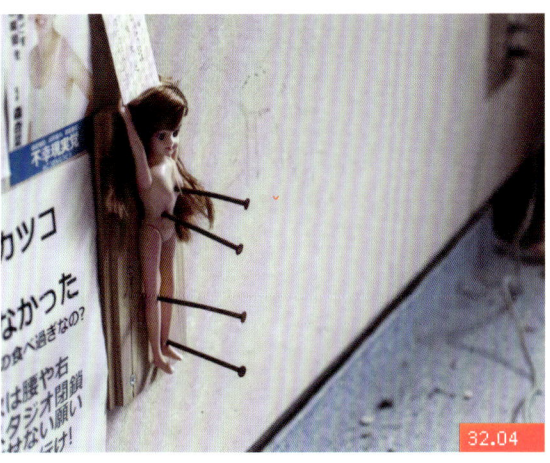

▶ 32.06
▶ 32.07

32.03
32.04
32.05

✠ Bizarre
※ Strange Cult's Bra Temple
◎ Asia
※ 2016

Location Classified

211

Project UrbEx

Location Classified

32.06 – 32.08
All the sheets of paper bear the same woman's name, while all the bras are exactly the same size. What was going on here?

32.09 – 32.10
Exit through the gift shop? As well as housing a completely different cult, this site retained the trappings of a temple. Weird.

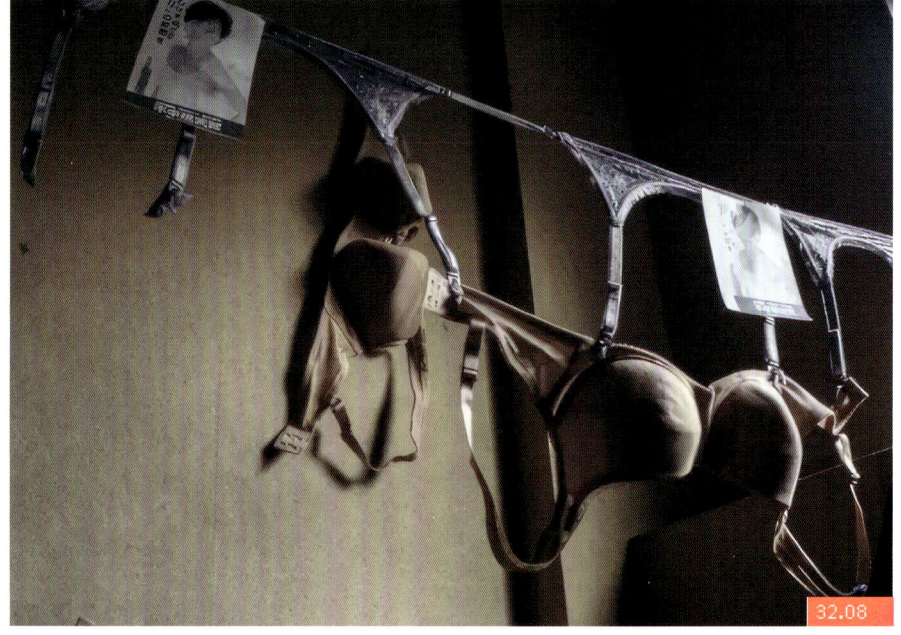

214　　　　　　　　　Project UrbEx

Location Classified

解説 # Soviet-era Flight School
A military base, Europe

For much of the 20th century, this would have been a high-security military base. Unauthorized visitors, especially ones wearing gas masks and speaking Japanese, would have been shouted at by sentries, barked at by guard dogs and possibly even shot. Yet my only challenge was sneaking past an old man who was sunbathing naked. How times change...

Originally a flight school training Luftwaffe pilots during the Second World War, the fortunes of conflict left this area occupied by Soviet troops. Sealed behind the Iron Curtain as part of East Germany during the Cold War, it became a military base for the 'other side' – Russia and its allies.

Then, in 1992, when East and West Germany became a single country once more, ownership of the base changed one more time.

▶33.10 Such a complex history literally left its mark, with wall paintings everywhere. ▶ Most were so heavily damaged by the time I explored the flight school in 2016 that I had to imagine how they must have looked.

It was obvious that all presented different visions of the perfect Soviet state. Red Army soldiers marching forever onwards as cosmonauts above them won the space race. I left here with a strong impression of how powerful and feared the Soviet Union had once been.

Not now, though. Weeds had taken over, with many structures in a horrible condition. However, this sprawling area remained an impressive part of history, even in this quiet, abandoned state.

✕ Military
※ Soviet-era Flight School
◎ Europe
※ 2016

33.01 – 33.03
What, no planes? Since becoming a pilot requires brains as well as *Top Gun* reflexes, trainees came here to do all the book stuff.

216 Project UrbEx

33.04 – 33.06
Even from the outside, it looked far more like a small college campus than a military base (it was both, more or less).

Location Classified

33.07 – 33.09
This location was so unvisited that it seemed as though each flake of paint that had fallen from the walls lay there, undisturbed...

33.10 – 33.11
...and what a lot of flakes that was. Military murals, once so proudly patriotic, had come apart like Communist-era jigsaw puzzles.

33.12
For the generation that grew up on both sides of the Iron Curtain, the Soviet Union seemed so. powerful... until the day it wasn't.

218   Project UrbEx

Location Classified 219

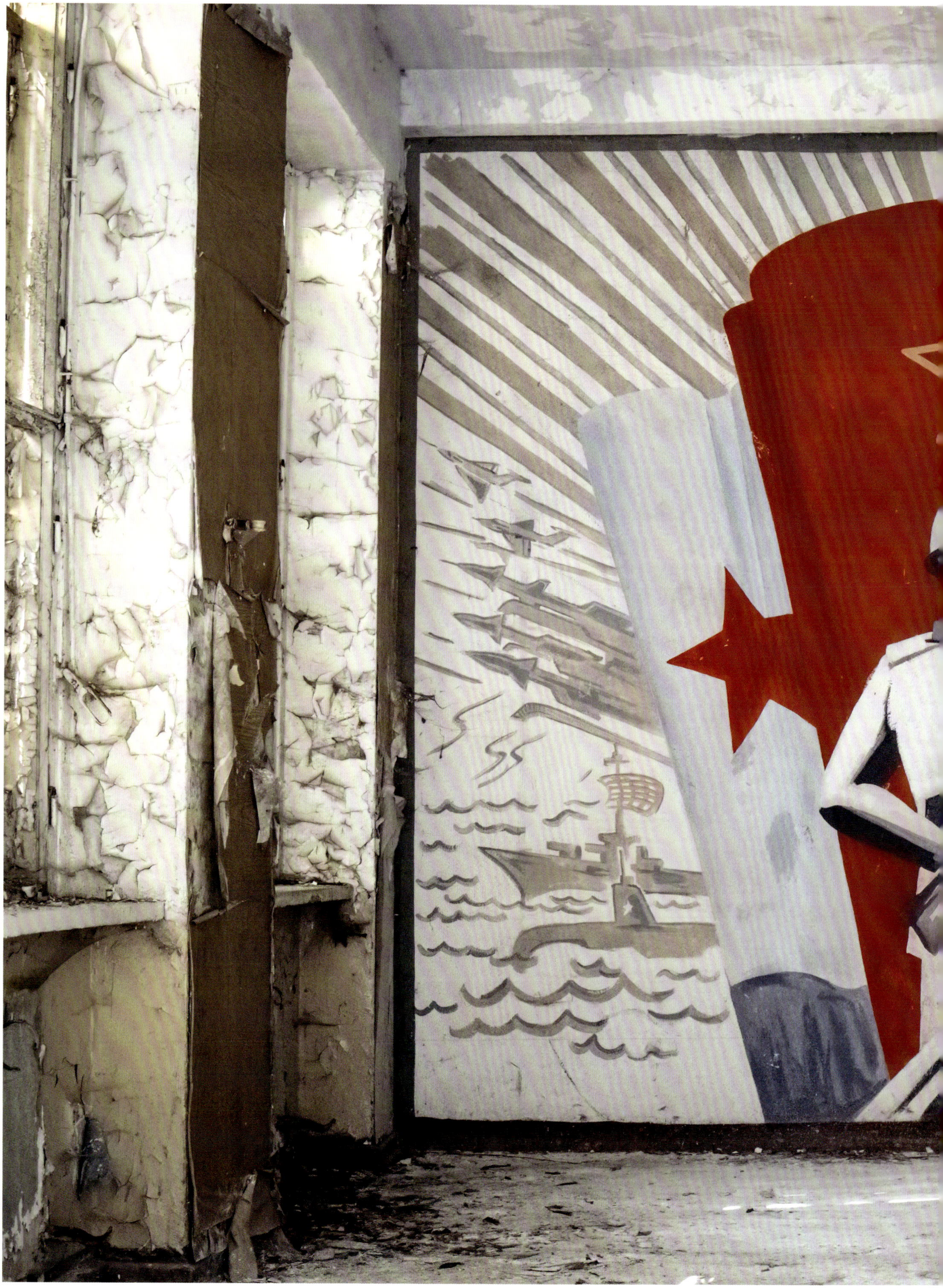

Location Classified

It's the worst-kept secret in the world but shhhh... life's a lot more fun when you make a game out of it. I know it because in my day job, I literally make games, while in my own time, I have the best time I can seeing the most incredible places out there...

"IT'S LIKE 'SILENT HILL' !!"

Project UrbEx

"IT'S LIKE 'THE LAST OF US' !!!"

...but if you know who I am then you must play games too, right? Whether it's beating your high score time on your walk to work or stealthing past the guy on the street holding a camera, I hope you'll always make your own fun wherever you go.

Ikumi Nakamura is an independent creative, explorer and videogame designer. Since 2004 she has photographed abandoned and uninhabited places and spaces across Europe, Asia and the North America to find inspiration for her games. Influenced by the videogame *S.T.A.L.K.E.R.*, she created a mysterious style of wearing a hoodie and gas mask when exploring. She also aspires to become a secrets hunter on the Japanese TV show *Discovery of the World's Mysteries*. The experiences and records of her photography pursuits are published on www.tomboy-urbex.com

Liam Wong is an award-winning freelance art director, graphic designer, former game developer, and photographer. He is best known for defining, designing and directing visual identities and has been listed as one of *Forbes* magazine's influential 30 under 30.

Front cover image: © Ikumi Nakamura

First published in the United Kingdom in 2023 by Read-Only Memory, an imprint of Thames & Hudson Ltd

This edition published in the United Kingdom in 2024 by Thames & Hudson Ltd, 181A High Holborn, London WC1V 7QX

First published in the United States of America in 2024 by Thames & Hudson Inc., 500 Fifth Avenue, New York, New York, 10110

Project UrbEx © 2023 Thames & Hudson Ltd, London

The text for this book was written by Cam Winstanley, based on interviews with Ikumi Nakamura.
Text © Cam Winstanley
Foreword © Liam Wong
Photographs © 2023 Ikumi Nakamura
Manga illustrations © 2023 Mai Mattori
Interior layout by Cantina

All Rights Reserved. No part of this publication may be reproduced or transmitted in any form or by any means, electronic or mechanical, including photocopy, recording or any other information storage and retrieval system, without prior permission in writing from the publisher.

British Library Cataloguing-in-Publication Data
A catalogue record for this book is available from the British Library.

Library of Congress Control Number 2023936952

ISBN 978-0-500-02694-6

Printed in China by RR Donnelley

Be the first to know about our
new releases, exclusive content
and author events by visiting
thamesandhudson.com
thamesandhudsonusa.com
thamesandhudson.com.au